KIRKPATRICK'S

FOUR LEVELS
of TRAINING
EVALUATION

JAMES D. and WENDY KAYSER
KIRKPATRICK

PRESS

ATD Press is an internationally renowned source of insightful and practical information
on talent development, training, and professional development.

ATD Press
1640 King Street
Alexandria, VA 22314 USA

Ordering information: Books published by ATD Press can be purchased by visiting ATD's
website at www.td.org/books or by calling 800.628.2783 or 703.683.8100.

Library of Congress Control Number: 2016935910

ISBN-10: 1-60728-008-6
ISBN-13: 978-1-60728-008-8
e-ISBN: 978-1-60728-102-3

ATD Press Editorial Staff
Director: Kristine Luecker
Manager: Christian Green
Associate Director, Communities of Practice: Justin Brusino
Community of Practice Manager, Learning & Development: Amanda Smith
Developmental Editor: Kathryn Stafford
Text Design: North Market Street Graphics
Cover Design: Jeff Miller, Faceout Studio

Printed by Data Reproductions Corporation, Auburn Hills, MI

Bonnie

Contents

Part 4: Case Studies   155

Chapter 17: Common Practice in Leadership Program: Greencore Northampton   157

Chapter 18: Service Over and Above the Rest (SOAR) Program: Emirates Airline   167

Chapter 19: Sales Graduate Program Pilot: ArjoHuntleigh Getinge Group   174

Foreword by Don Kirkpatrick

(as expressed to Jim Kirkpatrick)

Dear Reader,

The foreword you are about to read is the last that we will have from my dear dad, Don Kirkpatrick. I wrote his words as he dictated them to me during his final days. I hope that you will take to heart his last wishes for the training industry, which he asked me to share with you.

Sincerely,
Jim Kirkpatrick

Greetings,

I am pleased that my original book, *Evaluating Training Programs*, first published in 1993, is being replaced by an updated work. Jim and Wendy, my oldest son and daughter-in-law, are writing it. They have taken the model to depths I never dreamed of, calling it the New World Kirkpatrick Model. They explained to me many of the updates that you will learn about in this book: the end is the beginning, required drivers, business partnerships, and leading indicators.

I would like to say some things about training evaluation and my model. First, the legacy I leave will be the four levels, not me. I am glad that I got to meet many of you, and some of you enjoyed the way I taught the four levels (with my overhead projector and Packer song). My wish for you is that you find ways to use the model to better train people, that it improves the way they do their work, and that it ultimately contributes to the goals of your organization.

I also hope you acknowledge and remember the power of genuine person-to-person interaction in training and evaluation. Surveys and technology are fine, but the bridges that you build with your trainees and their managers, and the conversations you have with them, will add humanness to training content and evaluation data.

I am tired, my precious wife, Fern, has passed away, and I have given all I have to give. I am so very thankful for Wendy and Jim and the rest of my family, and for all of you who use my four levels.

I leave you with the last stanza of a poem that I think will encourage you:

> *I shall be telling this with a sigh*
> *Somewhere ages and ages hence:*
> *Two roads diverged in a wood, and I—*
> *I took the one less traveled by,*
> *And that has made all the difference.*

(ROBERT FROST, 1916)

Don Kirkpatrick
1924–2014

Foreword by Elaine Biech

It was 1954, and Dr. Donald Kirkpatrick was completing his dissertation. To hear him tell the story of the creation of the four levels, listeners could be lulled into believing that it wasn't a big deal. But it was a big deal—a really big deal.

Little did Don know the impact he would create with those four functional words:

- Reaction
- Learning
- Behavior
- Results

The four levels are pragmatic and straightforward. The simplicity of the Kirkpatrick Model has stood the test of time. Its practicality provides the profession with a logical approach to driving and evaluating the results of training and development.

The four levels and I go way back. Don Kirkpatrick and I both lived in Wisconsin, and we Wisconsinites are generally proud of our heritage. Don and I cheered for the Packers and the Badgers together. We ate thick, juicy burgers from the grill and gabbed about fishing on his boat. Since we both worked in the field of training and development (T&D), conversation always came around to evaluation. Don was adamant that the four levels were simply inevitable. He didn't like much attention and scoffed at being called a legend. He believed, in his unassuming way, that what he did was simply a matter of necessity; he created a method so the profession could evaluate the results of training and development.

Years later, Don, his son Jim, and daughter-in-law Wendy worked together to leverage Don's original work. Their meaningful, ground-breaking discussions led to the creation of the New World Kirkpatrick Model. Let's explore how the three Kirkpatricks expanded the model and why evaluation is critical to you and the future of the training industry.

ADDIE and Evaluation

Evaluation has always taken a back seat to training. It's the last thing most of us think about. Let's examine ADDIE, the instructional systems design (ISD) model that most of us use. A-D-D-I-E. There it is. E. Evaluate. Right at the end of the most important T&D acronym. Most of us know that a critical part of our job is to be able to *evaluate* our results. If you are effective, you evaluate, but you will be less effective if you wait until the end of ADDIE to consider what you will evaluate.

Let's review the ADDIE model to see how evaluation plays a valuable role in every ADDIE phase.

A—Analysis

This is the phase during which designers clarify the expectation—exactly what business result does the organization need to accomplish? What is the expected new behavior? What will it take to make those behaviors occur? How will we measure these things? To help define the design, you identify targeted business objectives, evaluate job performance, existing courses, task functions, learner characteristics, the timeline, learning constraints, and a host of other inputs to ensure you are on the right path.

To be truly effective, you must begin the *evaluation* process in the Analysis phase. The New World Kirkpatrick Model emphasizes identifying results (Level 4) up front. Identifying the *return on stakeholder expectations* provides indicators of value from a program or initiative. To identify specific measures, T&D professionals must ask questions to clarify and refine the expectations of key business stakeholders.

Questions include: What skills do your employees require? What should employees be doing on the job? What will cause them to perform those behaviors? What desired outcomes will your organization experience if these things occur?

These questions lead to observable, measurable business or mission outcomes and, of course, practical Levels 3 and 4 measures. When you think about it, this is the only way that makes sense! As Stephen Covey would say, "Plan with the end in mind."

D—Design

In this phase, designers write objectives, create evaluation tools, develop assessment instruments, determine media selection, and address other delivery details. Focusing on the shared requirements of the training department, supervisors and senior leaders ensure that the program will accomplish the desired return on stakeholder expectations.

For an effective design, you need to continue with the *evaluation* process in the design phase.

It is the best time to design your overall training strategy—planning what will occur before, during, and after training events. Evaluation is no exception to this rule. Determine what questions will be effective to measure Level 1 Reaction. What tests are needed to measure Level 2 Learning? What surveys or supervisory follow-up will effectively measure Level 3 Behavior change? Additionally, what methods of accountability and support will be designed for use after the training, and how will implementation be ensured? Finally, what tools will be best for gathering data to measure Level 4 Results? The answers to each of these questions supply data to determine whether the effort meets expectations.

D—Development

This is the phase during which learning and performance activities and materials are developed and instruction defined. Technology is also developed or integrated. Everything comes together in the development phase. Evaluation tools should be developed alongside the program materials.

The formative evaluation that occurs during this phase of instructional design helps to ensure that learners will reach the organization's performance and business objectives. This phase gives the designer an opportunity to validate and evaluate the instructional plans to ensure that the focus remains on the learner and the design leads to performance and results. This validation is often achieved by evaluating small-group trials. Evaluation in the development phase is directly related to the ultimate success of the training effort and determines whether it achieves the final expectations.

I—Implement

This phase includes the actual delivery of the learning and development, whether in an instructor-led virtual or traditional session, or in an asynchronous session. The learners have an opportunity to evaluate their experience using Level 1 Reaction and Level 2 Learning evaluations. Often these evaluations occur at the end of the class, but why wait until the end to evaluate?

You can obtain feedback and data on an ongoing basis so that you can make adjustments before it is too late. Even observing participants' behavior gives you clues about their satisfaction. Do they smile? Are they interested? Involved? Do they ask questions? Behavioral cues are good barometers; however, they give you incomplete feedback. Verify your impressions with an evaluation. To supplement an official Level 1 at the end of a section or a day, I like to give each participant an index card and ask them to rate the experience on a 1–7 scale, providing one reason they rated it as they did. Or you could ask them to complete a sentence, "I still need more information about . . ."

In a deeper, more strategic sense, implementation also includes follow-up after training. This broader view of implementation including Levels 1–3 drives performance instead of simply confirming readiness.

It's easy to connect *evaluation* with the implement phase. Remember, though, that you do not need to wait until the end.

E—Evaluate

This phase occurs continuously throughout the first four phases. If you've done your job all the way through the ADDIE model, evaluation becomes a placeholder at this point. It serves to remind you that it's not over until you can demonstrate that the effort meets expectations. That means that you must stay involved by connecting with supervisors and monitoring progress.

Evaluation is often viewed as a final step, but in actuality, what I'm stressing is that it starts the ADDIE process and plays a role in every phase along the way. The E doesn't belong just at the end; it belongs in every phase. Perhaps ADDIE should be $A_e\, D_e\, D_e\, I_e\, E$ to demonstrate that evaluation is a critical sub-step in each phase.

Whether you use the ADDIE model as prescribed or some other ISD version, you will be more effective and efficient if you evaluate within every phase. Evaluation is a critical step that should not be relegated to the end of the ADDIE process.

Embrace Evaluation

Finally, why should you care? What is the big deal about evaluation? Well, it is the one way that you can ensure that your organization sits up and takes notice of you and your department. When you focus on Level 4 Results, you determine organizational needs and identify performance gaps that may prevent the achievement of the results your organization requires. Conducting an organizational needs analysis and deciding what behavior at Level 3 is required to achieve the results is your road to success. Accelerate your results by using effective measures that drive and evaluate the performance and results and show that you have achieved a return on stakeholders' expectations. Demonstrating a return on the investment of training through evaluation is your route toward a true business partnership within your organization.

Embrace evaluation. It is training and development's bottom line.

Yes, the four levels have stood the test of time, becoming the most widely used training evaluation model in the world over the last 60-plus years. When I facilitate train-the-trainer sessions, I love the evaluation section. Why? Because when I ask the participants how many have heard of Kirkpatrick's four levels, almost all raise their hands. And when I ask them to recite the four levels, over half can state them accurately. Unfortunately, how they implement the four levels may vary widely—often not as effectively as the model could be implemented. Although Don died in 2014, the impact of his four words—Reaction, Learning, Behavior, Results—and the spirit of his work lives on through Jim and Wendy as they share the New World Kirkpatrick Model with all of us.

Don, Jim, and Wendy expanded the original model to create a powerful methodology—one that melds people with the metrics. Whenever I work with the Kirkpatricks their extensive knowledge about and their deep passion for our profession astounds me. They truly understand that evaluation is not just about analytics and metrics. It is more about the human spirit behind the measures and the need for consistent human interface along the way. The four levels are better than ever!

This book presents the most effective and logical evaluation approach. Jim and Wendy show you how to achieve the most from your evaluation practices. They address some of the Kirkpatrick myths. Most important, they present you with a clear plan to create and demonstrate training's value to your organization. Jim and Wendy present a pragmatic, as well as contemporary, approach to evaluating training. I will be surprised if you do not learn something new as you read about the realistic New World Kirkpatrick Model.

Elaine Biech
Norfolk, VA
April 2016

Preface

It is a humbling honor and a challenge to attempt to fill the shoes of our late father and father-in-law, Dr. Don Kirkpatrick. Don created what is now known as the Kirkpatrick Model, or the four levels, as the basis of his PhD dissertation at the University of Wisconsin in the 1950s. He was subsequently asked to describe these techniques for evaluating training programs in a series of four articles in 1959, which appeared in the *Journal of the American Society of Training Directors*.

From there, thousands of training professionals around the world read the articles and implemented the principles in their work. Because Don never established a business entity or actively promoted his model, use grew organically. It is quite a testament to the model that without sales, marketing, products, or any fanfare, it became the most widely used training evaluation model in the world.

The content in this book has been in the making for nearly 60 years. Over the course of those decades, Don's oldest son, Jim, was using and experimenting with the model in his own work as a training director and later as a consultant. Through this application and in using his expertise in education and psychology, it became clear that the model was not being implemented in a way that would maximize on-the-job application and subsequent business results. Several misassumptions and faulty practices were the culprits. Since the model was left to morph and be interpreted by each individual user for several decades, suffice it to say there are numerous variations as well as misconceptions about its application that are readily available on the Internet, in books, and in presentations around the world.

We have observed that many training professionals say they are "using Kirkpatrick," yet are following dated practices that are failing to create and demonstrate organizational value with their training. We tried to finesse these recommendations over the years, but three years ago decided to help put these changes on the fast track. We felt it was time to set the record straight by writing a book with a more complete description of the model and how to properly apply it in today's work environment. Thus, we introduce you to the New World Kirkpatrick Model. For those of you who have struggled with "getting to Levels 3 and 4," the concepts, principles, and techniques found in this book will now allow you to do so without breaking the budget.

The good news about Jim's decades of application and Wendy's more recent efforts is that they also uncovered and developed practical new truths and processes that maintain the four levels as the most popular evaluation model in the world. While the original four levels live on, the manner in which they are implemented is significantly different than what was outlined in earlier editions. This book is a necessary update to every training professional's library.

We are so grateful for the wonderful support we have received from the training industry in general as we carry on Don's work and show the timeless relevance of the simple and elegant principles he introduced more than 60 years ago. In particular, we would like to thank ATD Press for partnering with us on this.

We would also like to thank the contributors to this book. It takes a lot of time, and it also takes bravery to step up and share personal experiences in a way that puts them out there for others to analyze and critique. Without these examples, the principles just don't mean as much.

We also want to give special thanks to the editorial team, both within Kirkpatrick Partners and at ATD Press. Early in our marriage, when we were writing our first book together, Wendy said, "I won a writing contest in 7th grade." Jim said, "I got an F+ in English. The professor knew I tried really hard, so that was why he added the plus." Suffice it to say, writing a book with one's spouse is not the easiest of endeavors.

Finally, we want to thank those of you who have helped us uncover, develop, and fine-tune these concepts and principles into real-world successes. The New World Kirkpatrick Model came primarily from our working with L&D practitioners from the real world of work rather than from the privacy and comforts of our offices in Georgia. Those who have climbed the mountain before you now light the way for all to benefit.

We sincerely hope you find this book practical and applicable to your work. We also love to hear from you! Please tell us how you are using it, and perhaps you will be featured in a future piece.

Jim and Wendy Kirkpatrick
Newnan, GA
April 2016

PART 1

Basics of Evaluation

Part 1 explains the urgent need to evaluate training programs to maximize and demonstrate their value to the organization. In this section the four levels are introduced. Created in the 1950s by the late Dr. Donald Kirkpatrick, they form the most-used training evaluation model in the world.

The New World Kirkpatrick Model, introduced in 2009, builds on and modernizes the four levels to maximize their effectiveness in today's business world. The model, which forms the basis of the advice offered in this book, is outlined in chapter 2.

Before training can be evaluated, however, it is important that it is designed well from the start, so that there is some value to evaluate and report. Chapters 3 and 4 provide practical guidance for creating an effective evaluation strategy for any program or initiative. Even those who are educated in classic training evaluation principles are surprised by the modern, practical approach of the New World Kirkpatrick Model.

CHAPTER 1

Reasons for Evaluating

Maxine, a training specialist with a major corporation for seven years, could not believe her eyes as she read the letter that the human resources representative had just handed to her:

> *The Training Specialist position has been eliminated as part of a necessary reduction in force to align company resources with business needs. Your last day of employment is today . . .*

Maxine liked her job in the training department. She really felt that she had helped the business by creating good training programs and was particularly surprised to receive the notice because she had never said no to any training request sent her way. She thought she was a great team player.

How did Maxine get blindsided in this way? The reasons for evaluating training can shed some light on what happened.

The Urgent Need to Create and Demonstrate Training Value

Around the world, training and development is in a state of crisis. Training budgets are among the first to be cut when economic times get tough, and it's no wonder—training departments often see training as an end unto itself, rather than something that is simply a contributor to on-the-job performance. This lack of connection to performance and accomplishing key organizational results puts training into the "nice to have" category, instead of something that is required for organizational success. Failure to make a strong business case for training as something that is required to enhance performance and to measurably contribute to the most important organizational outcomes has left training in a precarious position.

Training professionals who think only about training events and not what happens before and particularly after them will become extinct. They are already being replaced by inexpensive off-the-shelf and outsourced training. These will probably be no more effective, but they are less expensive and will likely be equally effective.

Whether you're one of the in-house survivors or a struggling consultant, no training professional can coast indefinitely on lofty notions about continuous learning and employee development. Training professionals should question the purpose behind all training, even if it is requested or budgeted. There should be a conversation about the specific result that the training should support, and what the targeted group will have to do on the job to accomplish it.

You need to provide compelling evidence that training delivers bottom-line results and contributes to mission accomplishment. Training must reinvent itself and transcend the classroom to earn its budget and maintain its existence. Savvy business professionals and enlightened organizations know that training has little value unless what is learned gets applied on the job, and the subsequent on-the-job performance contributes to key organizational outcomes.

This book will explain how to create and implement an effective training evaluation strategy to fit and drive your training and performance initiatives, whether formal or informal, so that you can help to create and demonstrate the organizational value of your work. An effective strategy will ensure that your valuable, limited resources are dedicated to the programs and interventions that will bring about the most impact.

Employing these principles in your work will earn you a seat at the proverbial table with business executives and secure your future as a valuable resource and key partner in accomplishing organizational results. Training evaluation can be intimidating for some training professionals; fortunately, this book will use the Kirkpatrick Model, a straightforward, four-level approach that is elegant in its simplicity, making it equally straightforward to understand and implement. The Kirkpatrick Model is founded on the belief that training professionals can create and demonstrate the organizational value of their training without hiring costly outside consultants. The aim of both the model and this book is to show you how to do it yourself, with whatever resources you possess.

It is also important to note that the use of the word *training* relates to more than traditional classroom training. In the context of this book, it may be used to describe classroom training, e-learning, informal learning, social learning, or any type of modality in which individuals gain knowledge or skills to do their jobs more effectively.

Three Reasons to Evaluate Training Programs

There are three major reasons to evaluate training programs:

1. to improve the program
2. to maximize transfer of learning to behavior and subsequent organizational results
3. to demonstrate the value of training to the organization.

Evaluating to Improve the Program

Most training professionals are accustomed to evaluating training programs for the purpose of improving the program. Using formative (during the program) and summative (after the program) methods, they ask questions related to how participants enjoyed the program, whether they learned key information, and how the program might be improved for future sessions. This type of information is useful to learning and performance professionals to gauge the quality of their training programs, materials, and presenters. If evaluation of the training program shows that the program was well received and key information was learned, then the program can be called effective training.

Effective training: Well-received training that provides relevant knowledge and skills to the participants and the confidence to apply them on the job

---

Effective training is likely what many training professionals feel they are charged to deliver, and perhaps what is literally included in their job descriptions. However, most organizations are actually expecting more from the training department; they are expecting what is learned in training to be implemented on the job, and the implementation to make a measurable difference in key organizational results.

Returning to Maxine's story will punctuate the importance of going beyond simply providing effective training. About six months prior, Maxine was called to a meeting with Bernie, the sales manager. Bernie said that sales were down, so some product knowledge training should be conducted the following month in an off-site, one-day training event.

Maxine took the bait. She accepted the assignment and returned to her office to begin designing some product training, pulling from existing resources and developing others. After all, her job description was to deliver training to support company goals.

Sound familiar? This type of training order occurs around the globe daily.

The problem was that Maxine had no idea what was causing sales to drop, and she had no idea if lack of product knowledge was part of the cause. She designed and delivered a wonderful, effective training program. She confirmed that each sales rep had good product knowledge before leaving the program, and she reported these findings promptly to Bernie a few days after the event.

Unbeknown to Maxine, sales not only did not increase after training, they actually continued to drop. Bernie knew there were probably multiple causes, but he ultimately viewed the training as part of the problem. Unfortunately, the sales decrease was actually not due to a lack of sales representative product knowledge, so the training was a waste of resources.

This brings us to our next purpose of training evaluation.

Evaluating to Maximize Transfer of Learning to Behavior and Subsequent Organizational Results

More savvy training professionals realize that even the most well-designed and well-received training programs are of little use unless what is learned in training is relevant and gets implemented on the job. This is often called the transfer of learning to behavior. It is here where deliberate implementation of the Kirkpatrick Model will actually help to increase the degree of on-the-job application and, thus, impact to the business or organizational mission. If what was learned translates into improved job performance, then it is possible for better organizational results to be achieved. If training evaluation shows that on-the-job performance increased and results improved, then training effectiveness has occurred.

Training effectiveness: Training and follow-up leading to improved job performance that positively contributes to key organizational results

---

Returning to our story about Maxine and Bernie's sales training: Maxine could have done a lot more for her organization by having a conversation with Bernie about his sales training request. She could have asked some probing questions about what Bernie thought might be causing the decrease in sales. She could have asked his permission to informally interview a handful of the reps to get their opinions. Ultimately, what she needed to find out was what needed to change in on-the-job performance to improve results; in this case, sales volume.

If Maxine could have gotten this information, she could have made sure prior to investing the time and resources in a training program that training was actually going to help solve the problem. She might have found out that product knowledge was not the issue at all; perhaps a competitor had recently entered the market, introducing competition that did not previously exist. In that case, training on how the competitor's product compared to the company's product and how to effectively sell the company's product might have been a better use of resources.

When training professionals get out of the training order-taking mode and instead consider training requests as an invitation to a conversation about increasing performance and maximizing results, the stage is set for training value, the situation that training professionals need to have occur.

After training professionals partner with the business and design, develop, deliver, and evaluate training that improves performance and results, the next thing they need to do is to show that value in terms that their stakeholders understand and appreciate.

Evaluating to Demonstrate the Value of Training to the Organization

One of the most common excuses L&D professionals use to refute the possibility of demonstrating value is, "There are just too many variables for us to demonstrate the value of our training." This book will eliminate this excuse going forward, and demonstrate how to turn this negative into a positive. Instead of attempting to isolate one factor in performance and business success (training), this model promotes the practice of demonstrating the *relative value of many components*. This, therefore, requires L&D professionals and functions to involve themselves in as many of those factors as possible. These include activities that occur prior to and after training.

Learning and performance professionals must be able to show the organizational value of their training. Like any other department in an organization, training is not exempt from showing how the resources allocated to them have been put to good use. By gathering data related to effective training and training effectiveness, learning and performance professionals can credibly show the value that training has brought to the organization.

For Maxine's training program to have been considered successful, she would have needed to be able to make the case that the training helped reps to better sell the product in the field, and that sales actually did increase as a result. This information does not magically reveal itself; Maxine would have needed to create and implement a plan to gather data to show the benefit of the training.

Later chapters of this book will outline which information is most relevant to different stakeholder groups, and how to present it to them in terms that are meaningful to each of them. On the surface, demonstrating the value of training to the organization may seem self-serving; however, it is necessary not only for a training department to sustain itself, but also to earn the respect of other departments and the entire organization.

Summary

Training is in a state of crisis. Over-reliance on the training event puts L&D professionals in danger of being replaced by technology. It is already happening to an alarming degree. There exists an urgent need to move beyond the event and become heavily involved in creating and demonstrating business value. Special emphasis must be put into pre- and post-training activities to earn a seat at the table with business executives.

There are three basic reasons to evaluate. First, it is important to ensure that training programs are developed and delivered in such a way as to maximize learning. Second, targeted post-training evaluation can actually help to increase the amount of on-the-job application. Finally, the ultimate intent of good evaluation is to demonstrate business or mission value. This is best done by determining the relative contribution of key success factors rather than isolating one.

CHAPTER 2

The New World Kirkpatrick Model—An Overview

This chapter introduces the four levels, which form the basis of the most-used training evaluation model. This chapter also introduces the New World Kirkpatrick Model, which is the framework in which the four levels are implemented into today's work environment. The model presents the four levels in reverse, starting with Level 4, which is how the levels are considered when planning a program.

The Four Levels

The four levels were created by Dr. Don Kirkpatrick (1924–2014) in the 1950s as the subject of his dissertation. At the time, he was a professor at the University of Wisconsin. His focus was teaching management and supervisory programs for area businesses as part of a university educational outreach program. He genuinely wished to know if the training programs he conducted were making a difference for participants; hence, the four levels were born.

Don used the four levels to evaluate his own training programs. After his dissertation was published, he received a request from the organization now known as the Association for Talent Development (ATD) to write an article on the topic. Don wrote a series of four articles, entitled "Reaction," "Learning," "Behavior," and "Results." Training professionals around the world read the four articles and applied the principles in their work. Unbeknown to Don, these principles were coined the four levels, and the Kirkpatrick Model. As Don himself said many times, "I never called Reaction, Learning, Behavior, and Results the 'four levels,' but somebody did, and the words caught on. The next thing I learned was that training professionals were calling my four words the 'Kirkpatrick Model,' a term I had never used either."

The organic growth and use of the model worldwide between the 1950s and 1990s, when Don wrote his first book, *Evaluating Training Programs: The Four Levels,* is a testament to the practicality of the model. Absent any marketing, promotion, or support of a Kirkpatrick company, thousands of training professionals independently used and adapted the model to meet their needs. The definitions have changed slightly over the past decades; this book provides the latest wording (Table 2-1).

Table 2-1. The Four Levels

Level 1: Reaction	The degree to which participants find the training favorable, engaging and relevant to their jobs
Level 2: Learning	The degree to which participants acquire the intended knowledge, skills, attitude, confidence and commitment based on their participation in the training
Level 3: Behavior	The degree to which participants apply what they learned during training when they are back on the job
Level 4: Results	The degree to which targeted outcomes occur as a result of the training and the support and accountability package

The New World Kirkpatrick Model

The year 2009 marked the 50th anniversary of the four levels. Over the course of five decades, numerous circumstances changed in training and the workplace. In 2010, we enhanced the four levels to accomplish the following goals:

- Incorporate the forgotten or overlooked teachings of Dr. Kirkpatrick, Sr.
- Correct common misinterpretations and misuse of the model.
- Illustrate how the model applies to modern talent development and performance.

The New World Kirkpatrick Model honors and maintains the time-tested four levels and adds new elements to help people to operationalize them effectively in the new world of business, government, military, and not-for-profit organizations

(Figure 2-1). The advent of computers has created a generally faster pace of business; e-learning and online events have changed the face of training; easy access to information and learning on the Internet anytime someone wants it has changed how learning generally is viewed. The fact that the majority of learning takes place informally, on the job, has also been presented as a challenge for application of the four levels. The New World Model addresses this modernization of the working and learning landscape.

The New World Model also corrects misapplications that became common practice during the decades when training professionals used and adapted the model on their own, such as the over-emphasis on Levels 1 and 2, and the misguided belief that Levels 3 and 4 are too expensive or too difficult to evaluate.

Figure 2-1. The New World Kirkpatrick Model

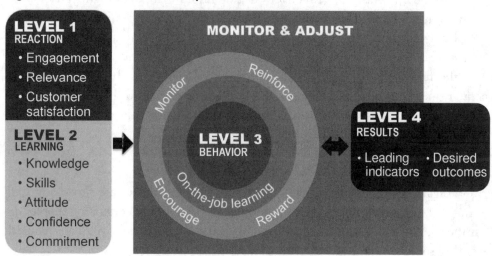

The Four Levels in Reverse

In this section, the four levels will be presented in the order in which you should consider them during the planning phase of a program, in reverse order from Level 4 to Level 1. This keeps the focus on what is most important, the program outcome that is accomplished through improved on-the-job performance of training graduates.

Once the training has been implemented and evaluation has actually occurred, the levels can be evaluated closer to their numerical order of 1–4, but not necessarily in a linear, sequential fashion.

Level 4: Results

Level 4 holds the distinction of being the most misunderstood of the four levels. It is the degree to which targeted outcomes occur as a result of the training and the support and accountability package.

Level 4: Results: The degree to which targeted outcomes occur as a result of the training and the support and accountability package

---

A common misapplication occurs when professionals or functional departments define results in terms of their small, individual area of the organization instead of globally for the entire company. This creates silos and fiefdoms that are counterproductive to organizational effectiveness. The resulting misalignment causes layers upon layers of dysfunction and waste.

Clarity regarding the true Level 4 result of an organization is critical. By definition, it is some combination of the organizational purpose and mission, combined with the financial reality of sustained existence and success. In a for-profit company, it means profitably delivering the product or service to the marketplace. In a not-for-profit, government, or military organization, it means accomplishing the mission while responsibly using the resources available.

Creating the Level 4 Result Statement

Every organization has just one Level 4 result. Business results are broad and long term. They are created through the culmination of countless efforts of people, departments, and environmental factors. They can take months or years to manifest. Here are some sample Level 4 result statements (Table 2-2).

Table 2-2. Sample Level 4 Result Statements

Training Company	Military Organization	Phone Company	Government Agency
Help other organizations to reach their highest goals through profitable growth of training products, programs, and services.	Protect our country's people and resources and promote worldwide peace.	Profitably provide the largest network to keep people connected to family, friends, and business.	Provide the highest level of service possible to citizens for their hard-earned tax dollars.

A good test of whether or not the correct Level 4 result has been identified is a positive answer to the question, "Is this what the organization exists to do, deliver, or contribute to its customers or society, at a high level?"

While this definition of results is straightforward, frustration with the seeming inability to relate a single training class to the organizational result is common.

Leading Indicators

There are, however, leading indicators that can help bridge the gap between individual initiatives and organizational results. These are short-term observations and measurements that suggest that critical behaviors are on track to create a positive impact on the desired results.

Leading Indicators: Short-term observations and measurements that suggest that critical behaviors are on track to create a positive impact on the desired results

---

Organizations will have a number of leading indicators that encompass departmental and individual goals, each contributing to the accomplishment of the highest-level result. Common examples of leading indicators include monthly sales volume, defective rate, employee retention, and customer satisfaction scores.

While leading indicators are important measurements, they must be balanced with a focus on the highest-level result. For example, a company with excellent customer satisfaction scores could go out of business if it does not maintain profitability, comply with laws and regulations, and keep its employees reasonably happy. Note that customer satisfaction is an example of a goal that does not provide an affirmative answer to the question, "Is this what the organization exists to contribute?" No organization exists simply to deliver customer service alone.

Numerous leading indicators align with the Level 4 result of an organization. Each leading indicator is just one step toward reaching the true target of organizational results, and this perspective must be maintained to achieve organizational alignment.

Level 3: Behavior

Level 3 is the degree to which participants apply what they learned during training when they are back on the job. The New World Level 3 Behavior consists of critical behaviors, required drivers, and on-the-job learning.

Level 3: Behavior: The degree to which participants apply what they learned during training when they are back on the job

Critical Behaviors

Critical behaviors are the few, specific actions, which, if performed consistently on the job, will have the biggest impact on the desired results.

 Critical behaviors: The few, key behaviors that the primary group will have to consistently perform on the job to bring about targeted outcomes

There are perhaps thousands of behaviors a given employee might perform on the job; critical behaviors are those that have been identified as the most important to achieving organizational success. Alignment of what is learned during training with critical behaviors and the desired leading indicators is the key to creating training programs that deliver value to the organization.

Required Drivers

The New World Kirkpatrick Model adds required drivers to Level 3. Required drivers are processes and systems that reinforce, monitor, encourage, and reward performance of critical behaviors on the job. Common examples of required drivers include job aids, coaching, work review, pay-for-performance systems, and recognition for a job well done.

 Required drivers: Processes and systems that reinforce, monitor, encourage, and reward performance of critical behaviors on the job

Required drivers are the key to accomplishing the desired on-the-job application of what is learned during training. They decrease the likelihood of people falling through the cracks, or deliberately crawling through the cracks if they are not interested in performing the required behaviors.

Organizations that reinforce the knowledge and skills learned during training with accountability and support systems can expect as much as 85 percent application on the job. Conversely, companies that rely primarily on training events alone to create good job performance achieve around a 15 percent success rate (Brinkerhoff 2006).

Active execution and monitoring of required drivers is perhaps the biggest indicator of program success for any initiative.

On-the-Job Learning

On-the-job learning is part of the New World Level 3 in recognition of two facts of the modern workplace:

1. Up to 70 percent of all learning that directly contributes to job performance takes place on the job.
2. Personal responsibility and motivation are key partners to external support and reinforcement efforts for optimal performance.

Creating a culture and expectation that individuals are responsible for maintaining the knowledge and skills to enhance their own performance will encourage individual accountability and empowerment. On-the-job learning provides an opportunity for employees and their employers to share the responsibility for good performance.

Level 2: Learning

The definition of Level 2 Learning is the degree to which participants acquire the intended knowledge, skills, attitude, confidence and commitment based on their participation in the learning event (Table 2-3). Confidence and commitment have been added to Level 2 in the New World Kirkpatrick Model to close the gap between learning and behavior, as well as to prevent the cycle of waste when training is repeated for people who possess the required knowledge and skills but fail to perform appropriately on the job.

Level 2: Learning: The degree to which participants acquire the intended knowledge, skills, attitude, confidence and commitment based on their participation in the training

---

Table 2-3. Level 2 Learning Components

Knowledge:	*"I know it."*
Skill:	*"I can do it right now."*
Attitude:	*"I believe this will be worthwhile to do on the job."*
Confidence:	*"I think I can do it on the job."*
Commitment:	*"I will do it on the job."*

Knowledge and Skill

Knowledge is the degree to which participants know certain information, as characterized by the phrase, "I know it."

Skill is the degree to which they know how to do something or perform a certain task, as illustrated by the phrase, "I can do it right now."

Many organizations make the common and costly mistake of inaccurately diagnosing poor performance as a lack of knowledge or skill. Underachievers are continually returned to training with the belief that they do not know what to do, when in reality, the more common cause of substandard performance is a lack of motivation or other environmental factors.

Attitude

Attitude is defined as the degree to which training participants believe that it will be worthwhile to implement what is learned during training on the job. Attitude is characterized by the phrase, "I believe this will be worthwhile to do on the job." It is important to note that this definition of attitude does not necessarily mean that the individual has changed his attitude about a given topic; rather, it means that the individual sees the importance of doing what is asked on the job, based on the expressed benefits of compliance or penalties for noncompliance.

For example, an organization may have a diversity-awareness program. The program is unlikely to actually change a participant's long-held attitude about people of different ages, genders, or religions. However, the program could influence the participant to see the importance of treating all people equally at work to avoid disciplinary action or dismissal for prejudicial actions.

Confidence

Confidence is defined as the degree to which training participants think they will be able to do what they learned during training on the job, as characterized by the phrase, "I think I can do it on the job."

Addressing confidence during training brings learners closer to the desired on-the-job performance. It can proactively surface potential on-the-job application barriers so they can be resolved.

Commitment

Commitment is defined as the degree to which a learner intends to apply the knowledge and skills learned during training to the job. It is characterized by the phrase, "I will do it on the job." Commitment relates to learner motivation by acknowledging that even if the knowledge and skills are mastered, effort still must be put forth to use the information or perform the skills on a daily basis.

Level 1: Reaction

Don Kirkpatrick referred to Level 1 as the customer satisfaction measurement of training. The New World Kirkpatrick definition of Level 1 Reaction is the degree to which participants find the training favorable, engaging and relevant to their jobs. Due to the likelihood that Level 1 will be evaluated for most training, this provides additional components and heightened importance of the data collected.

Level 1: Reaction: The degree to which participants find the training favorable, engaging and relevant to their jobs

---

Approximately 80 percent of live classroom programs and 58 percent of electronically delivered programs are evaluated at Level 1 in some fashion. The current investment in gathering this type of data is far greater than the importance this level dictates. This investment occurs at the cost of evaluating Level 3, which would yield data more meaningful to the business and is only evaluated for 33 percent of live classroom programs and 17 percent of electronically delivered programs (ATD 2016).

Customer Satisfaction

One of the least important program components, customer satisfaction tends to be overly emphasized in current evaluation practice. With that said, customer satisfaction does have a positive correlation to learning, so some degree of satisfaction is beneficial. The current problem is the amount of evaluation resources used to summatively evaluate this dimension, at a point when little or nothing can be done to improve it.

A more purposeful approach to evaluating customer satisfaction would be to use it to formatively identify and eliminate any barriers to learning during the program.

Engagement

Engagement refers to the degree to which participants are actively involved in and contributing to the learning experience. Engagement levels directly relate to the level of learning that is attained.

Program interest is most commonly the focus of participant engagement evaluation efforts; for example, how the facilitator involved and captivated the audience. However, personal responsibility, or how present and attentive participants were during the training, is arguably a more important part of engagement.

Relevance

Relevance is the degree to which training participants will have the opportunity to use what they learned in training on the job. Relevance is important to ultimate training value because even the best training is a waste of resources if the participants have no application for the content in their everyday work.

Many people have also experienced a situation in which training is done too far in advance of the likely application timeline, which reduces its relevance.

Monitor and Adjust

The large box labeled Monitor and Adjust in the New World Kirkpatrick Model diagram represents the role of the training function during major initiatives after formal training is complete. During this time period, training professionals should track on-the-job performance and implementation of required drivers at Level 3, as well as status of leading indicators at Level 4, to see if the initiative is moving in the right direction. If not, analysis needs to be done as to why, and adjustments made to the on-the-job activities.

Be sure to identify those individuals and areas exhibiting above-standard performance and to reinforce and leverage those best practices. Make no mistake—the real power of any initiative is found in this section of the model. This is where program success occurs or not.

It is important to note that the New World Model is not a full feedback loop. The reason is because when desired program outcomes are not achieved, the cause is usually found on the job, not in a lack of knowledge or skill. It is seldom necessary to send employees back to the classroom. Interventions within the Monitor and Adjust portion of the model will almost always remove the barriers to success and keep the program on track to produce the desired results.

Summary

Levels 1 and 2 of the New World Kirkpatrick Model provide data related to effective training. These measurements are useful primarily to the training function to internally measure the quality of the programs they design and deliver.

Levels 3 and 4 provide data related to training effectiveness, which is typically the type of data that stakeholders find valuable.

The New World Model diagram illustrates that no shortcut exists from Levels 1 and 2 straight through to Level 4. The required on-the-job level of effort must be discussed to maximize the results of your initiatives. This is a critical conversation because the organization often wants to put the sole responsibility of solving business problems on training, but these problems cannot be solved with training alone.

The simplicity of the original four levels is maintained in the New World Kirkpatrick Model to retain its timeless appeal, flexibility, and ease of implementation for all types of programs.

References

ATD Research. 2016. *Evaluating Learning: Getting to Measurements That Matter.* Alexandria, VA: ATD Press.

Brinkerhoff, R.O. 2006. *Telling Training's Story: Evaluation Made Simple, Credible, and Effective.* San Francisco, CA: Berrett-Koehler.

Levels 1 and 2 - effective training
Levels 3 and 4 - training effectiveness

CHAPTER 3

Developing an Effective
Evaluation Strategy

Before thinking about evaluating the effectiveness of a training program, you need to ensure that the program will actually provide some value. This chapter provides an overview of the important considerations to keep in mind when planning a program and related evaluation activities. Following the advice in this chapter will make the best use of your precious, limited resources.

A Cautionary Tale

Most training professionals are hungry for any guidance as to how to create and demonstrate the value of training to their organizations, and they fully understand that the risk of failing to do this may mean elimination of their funding, their department, and ultimately their jobs. Most training strategies consist of a survey at Level 1, pre- and post-tests at Level 2, and then hoping for the best. There is a gap between Levels 2 and 3, sometimes called the "great divide," which training professionals must bridge and cross. It is not much of an exaggeration to suggest that you need to be a civil engineer and work with the business to build the bridge that connects training to the business.

There are perhaps still a few training departments that believe they have a blank check and unlimited time to make their organizational contribution. If you are in this group, here is a cautionary tale.

Jim was invited to a technology company in Canada to do a workshop for the training group. The topic was the risk of failing to demonstrate the organizational value of training. Throughout the program, interest seemed low. When Jim probed a bit, one participant stood up and proclaimed, "Jim, we are the exception. Look around you. The organization built this campus for us because they know that we are bringing value."

Jim continued the workshop, but interaction was still lackluster. At the end of the presentation, Jim offered to send more information to those who left a business card. Just one woman shyly snuck him her card and slunk out of the room.

Six months later, the woman who provided the business card emailed Jim. "Remember those 100 people you spoke with a while ago? Seventy-five of them are gone." She went on to explain that leadership had said there was no evidence that the value that training had brought to the organization warranted the cost.

This is not an isolated incident; we could tell you more, similar stories. Do not let this happen to you and your department. This chapter provides guidance to create a credible program evaluation strategy.

Not All Programs Are Created Equal

Around the world, there is a common question about training evaluation: To what degree should each program be evaluated? The short answer is that the degree to which a program is evaluated should match its importance or cost to the organization. Not all programs are of equal importance, so it would be wasteful to fully evaluate a less essential program, and risky to not sufficiently evaluate a program that is mission critical for the organization.

Consider what information is useful to you, the training professional, and what information is required to be credible in the eyes of your stakeholders. Information useful to training professionals typically relates to Levels 1 and 2. You want to ensure that the training resulted in learning, and ultimately, that participants are ready to perform on the job. Information related to credibility typically relates to Levels 3 and 4. You need to convince stakeholders that training participants used what they learned on the job, performed better as a result, and positively affected key business metrics. Usefulness and credibility are your guides for what to evaluate, and to what degree.

Usefulness: Information used to make decisions related to the program

Credibility: Information demonstrating program value in business terms defined by stakeholders

---

It is usually obvious which programs are the most organizationally important. They are large in scale and expensive, and the stakes are high if they are unsuccessful.

They align most closely to corporate strategy and goals. Typical examples include onboarding, leadership development, new product launches, safety and security, and other major initiatives. These programs warrant a complete evaluation package, as outlined in this book.

Programs that are less mission critical do not require a full evaluation package. Examples include short training modules on company procedures and computer programs, communication skills and professional development offerings that are customized to the individual, and other programs not tied to major initiatives. For these programs, a practical approach to evaluation should be used in which you select just a few abbreviated evaluation methods and tools to ensure that the program results in the required learning, performance, and outcomes. For example, a one-hour course in word processing could include hands-on skills tests and a quiz to ensure that learning has occurred. After the program, a quick check could be done to ensure that graduates are using the program properly and completing work efficiently, accurately, and professionally.

Occasionally, an organization has trouble defining which programs and initiatives are the most important and warrant a complete evaluation plan. In such cases, the best approach is to talk with stakeholders and find out what they think is most important. If the list is more than a few "most important" programs, you may want to use the program impact rating tool to identify the small handful that really will create the most organizational impact if successful (Table 3-1).

Three Phases of a Program

To maximize an initiative's effectiveness and the value that can be reported to the organization, programs and the related evaluation activities should be viewed in three phases: planning, execution, and demonstration of value (Figure 3-1). Throughout this book, we will reference evaluation-related activities that should occur before, during, and after the training event or program. The primary focus of this book, however, is on the evaluation-related activities that occur during the execution phase.

Planning Phase

During the planning phase of a program or initiative, critical tasks must be performed that make it possible for the program to create organizational value. Training professionals would be wise to redefine their definition of training design and development to include more than just building the training program. It should also include creating the plans to prepare managers and participants for training, the

Table 3-1. Program Impact Rating Tool

Program	Strategic		Tactical					Comments
	Potential strategic impact	Executive interest / sponsorship / support	Managerial reinforcement and support	Availability of data (especially Level 4)	Access to training graduates	Realistic scope	Total tactical "Yes" responses	
Ex. Leadership at Acme	Yes	Yes	Yes	Yes	Yes	No	3	

Instructions: List each program that is viewed to be mission critical in the left column. For each strategic and tactical dimension, rate the program as a yes or no. If any program does not get a "yes" for both strategic dimensions, it is not a good candidate and should be crossed out. For the remaining programs, total up all of the "yes" responses to reach a score. The highest scores typically indicate the programs that are the best choices to fully evaluate.

post-training support and accountability package, and the evaluation tools that will be used throughout the program.

Training professionals should not be mere designers and developers of training content; they should view themselves as learning and performance architects, building a complete package.

Figure 3-1. Three Phases of a Program

Defining Program Outcomes

During the planning phase, first identify the true Level 4 result of the organization. Once you are clear on what your organization exists to do, then you need to talk with stakeholders about what this program or initiative is supposed to contribute to those results, or what leading indicators it will positively influence. This defines the expectations in the return on expectations (ROE) for the program, or what a successful training initiative delivers to key business stakeholders, demonstrating the degree to which their expectations have been satisfied.

Return on Expectations: What a successful training initiative delivers to key business stakeholders, demonstrating the degree to which their expectations have been satisfied

---

A common question about defining ROE is the degree to which specific targets are set or not for the targeted program outcomes. The answer is, it depends. Sometimes, the target is clear based on the program. For example, if an organization has experienced on-the-job injuries and has a mandated intervention, then the goal is likely no more injuries.

However, most initiatives are going to have more subjectivity. For example, an organization might be experiencing an undesirable level of employee turnover. It is tempting to try to set a target, but upon what would that target be based? Sometimes, it makes more sense to focus on building a strong implementation plan and simply monitoring the outcome to watch for improvement. Eventually, after data have been collected over a period of time, it may be realistic to quantify the expectations more specifically.

ROE is a key differentiator of the Kirkpatrick methodology. It is a proactive measurement of training value in that training professionals have to partner with the business before the training initiative even begins. Together, they determine what success will look like and how it will be measured, giving credit to all of the success factors that went into the collaborative effort.

Success factors: Items that each contribute to on-the-job application, performance, and ultimate results, including required drivers, the training program, personal responsibility, and necessities for success

---

Building this strategic bridge to program stakeholders opens lines of communication so that a good program plan can be created and executed together. The conversation centers on performance and results, more so than the means to an end that training provides.

The photograph of the rustic Scottish bridge illustrates our point (Figure 3-2). If formal training components are planned and executed well, resulting in strong Level 1 Reaction, it is very likely that Level 2 Learning will take place. This is a natural occurrence. Similarly, if the required driver package at Level 3 is executed in such a way as to achieve significant and sustained on-the-job application, it is quite likely that positive Level 4 leading indicators will occur. This is another naturally occurring sequence.

The problem is with the connection—or better, lack of connection—between Levels 2 and 3. There is almost no researched-based predictive connection between knowledgeable, skilled employees and actual on-the-job application. It must be built, and who better to initiate it than L&D? Note that the bridge in the photograph is the only human-made structure. Simply put, L&D needs to take the initiative and begin building that bridge through partnerships, policies, and cross-functional teams if there is to be any significant Level 3 application and subsequent Level 4 results.

ROE lies in contrast to return on investment (ROI), which attempts to isolate the value of the training program alone and is done after the fact. ROI is a defensive and reactive tactic that calls for little or no collaboration between training and the

Figure 3-2. Scottish Bridge

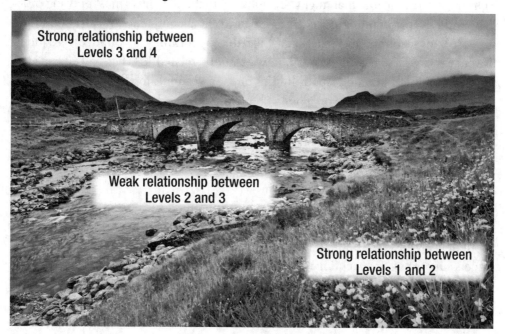

Strong relationship between Levels 3 and 4

Weak relationship between Levels 2 and 3

Strong relationship between Levels 1 and 2

© Xavier Arnau

business. Rather, there is more of an effort to separate the two so that training professionals can "take credit" for what they did without taking into account any efforts of business leaders, supervisors, training participants, and others who assisted with the support and accountability package after the training.

Identifying Critical Behaviors and Required Drivers

The next step in the planning process is to define what employees need to actually do on the job to maximize the organizational results that stakeholders wish to influence. This step can be surprisingly difficult, so it is important to build tactical bridges with line managers, supervisors, and top performers to discuss the required on-the-job performance.

Before asking for employee involvement, the key is to build mutual understanding and trust by showing an interest in their work needs, asking questions, listening, and ultimately using their language rather than training jargon.

Avoid phrases such as skills gaps, learning culture, learning objectives, and the four levels. Instead, ask employees about their goals and targets for the year. Ask what business challenges they are experiencing. Find out if performance in certain areas is reducing outcomes. Such conversations help your business partners to see that you have their employee performance and business goals at the root of what you propose.

Once you are clear on the critical behaviors, then you can discuss what types of interventions might solve the current performance problem or outcome shortfall. Training is only one tool that might be a solution to the business's most pressing problems. And even if training is necessary, it must be accompanied by a post-training support and accountability package. Take this opportunity to build the required drivers package together. Set specific expectations related to what will occur after training and the roles and responsibilities of each group. Literally set up the schedule of post-program discussion points about progress and any necessary modifications to keep the program on track to produce the desired outcomes. Building the post-program plan is arguably the most important part of the process.

Addressing Necessities for Success

Many worthy training initiatives fail because something in the workplace environment sabotages application efforts or is missing. For example, if employees learn about new processes in training, but return to work and hear managers and company leaders supporting or accepting use of the existing processes, chances of the new processes being used are small. Or, if there is an incentive system based purely on sales numbers while an initiative suggests that "relationships" are what is most important. True learning and performance professionals will call out these issues and discuss how to resolve them with stakeholders and line managers.

Ideally, learning professionals provide the suggested necessities for success to overcome these issues. Necessities for success are prerequisite items, events, or conditions that will help leverage success or head off problems before they reduce the impact of an initiative. Learning professionals should make it clear that these issues must be addressed and resolved prior to moving forward, or they will jeopardize the desired outcomes.

Necessities for success: Prerequisite items, events, conditions, or communications that will help leverage success or head off problems before they reduce the impact of an initiative

---

Designing the Intervention

The next step is to determine what training, if any, is required to support employees in performing the critical behaviors on the job to contribute to the key organizational results. This step is important: You may determine that training is not even necessary, or is not the best intervention to meet your goals.

It is very counterproductive for training professionals to make their tagline, "We provide learning solutions." It is too narrow, and it is not speaking the language of the business. As a learning and performance architect, you should be ready to recommend other types of interventions, such as process redesign or organizational alignment analysis.

Assuming that there is a definite need for knowledge or skills practice, then, and only then, should the training program design be initiated. The managers and supervisors of the intended training audience should be included in verifying that the program content is on target; ideally, they will actually participate as subject matter experts in the program design.

Designing the Evaluation Tools

During the planning phase, you also want to design and build the tools that will be used to evaluate the program as it is executed. For more than five decades, the learning and development community has been under the mistaken belief that most or all training evaluation activities occur at the end of the training process. Popular training models such as ADDIE (analyze, design, develop, implement, evaluate) perpetuate this false and counterproductive approach.

Evaluation is not an afterthought to training, but rather is meant to be integrated into the entire learning and development process. If you wait until after a program is designed, developed, and delivered to consider what value it is supposed to provide to the organization and how you will evaluate it, there is little chance of the program having much value.

Another important consideration when developing an evaluation strategy that will work in your organization is that more often than not, training and business professionals report that they are asked to do more with less. The greatest plan in the world is of no use if it is too complicated or costly to execute. Also consider your organizational culture. For example, if there is generally mistrust and blame, then individual interviews may not yield honest feedback and good testimonials. If the message is that managers are developers of their direct reports, then involving them in the evaluation is important.

Using Blended Evaluation® Tools

One of the most debilitating misconceptions of the four levels is that the proper way to address them is one level at a time, starting with Level 1 Reaction. This antiquated belief keeps many training professionals stuck at Levels 1 and 2, trying to defend the effectiveness of their training to a stakeholder audience that isn't terribly interested in the related data. The power is in connecting the levels, not keeping them separate. With this in mind, we have developed a Blended Evaluation® approach, which uses methods or tools that evaluate more than one level at the same time.

Blended Evaluation®: Evaluation methodology in which data are collected from multiple sources using multiple methods, in a fashion that considers all four Kirkpatrick levels

---

Executing a Blended Evaluation Plan maximizes program evaluation resources and assists in gathering robust data. Instead of "doing a Level 1" immediately after a training program, create a Blended Evaluation Form in which you include items related to Levels 1 and 2, as well as anticipated application and outcomes. In a delayed evaluation, you focus on how training graduates have applied what they learned, what support they are receiving on the job (Level 3), and what kinds of results they have accomplished (Level 4).

Using Actionable Intelligence

Another concept to keep in mind when designing your evaluation plan is actionable intelligence, which means being deliberate and purposeful about the evaluation data you collect, rather than just following tradition or doing what has always been done. Intelligent data collection means selecting methods that provide both qualitative and quantitative data that will be useful to you and meaningful to your stakeholders. For example, intelligent data could be that which would help you to enhance the program, remove a barrier to implementation on the job, or collect evidence of positive outcomes for stakeholders.

Frank Anderson, past president of the Defense Acquisition University, defined scrap training as any training that is not meaningful and does not contribute to Levels 3 and 4. Following suit, we coined the term *scrap evaluation* in 2012, defined as investing resources in evaluating data that is not useful to the training function to make good program decisions, nor meaningful to the stakeholders who want to see program results.

Execution Phase

The execution phase of an initiative includes not only the training program or event but also activities to prepare for the program and all subsequent support and accountability activities. Today, the time and effort spent on training program design and development dwarfs the time spent on post-training support. It is baffling that the training industry has not changed this dangerous pattern. This myopic view of training causes training jobs to be lost and training departments to be closed or outsourced.

Preparing Participants for Training

Managers and supervisors of training participants should be given materials and asked to introduce the training to their direct reports, outlining expectations for what should happen before, during, and after the program. For major initiatives, the support of senior leadership is often enlisted to position the program in a positive light and make it a priority.

Training participants should arrive at the training event with a positive, clear message as to the purpose of the training and what they are expected to do as a result of participating. This creates instant engagement because learners will know that it isn't a "flavor of the day" that will be forgotten the moment they leave the classroom or turn off their computers.

Tying Training to Performance During Training

During the training, the trainer should frequently refer to how the information will be used on the job and initiate discussion surrounding any concerns about implementing the ideas. Since critical behaviors and specific outcomes were defined in advance, they should actually be built right into the training program. Part of the trainer's role is to emphasize the relevance of the material to the participants, rather than simply hoping they see the connection.

Support and Accountability After Training

The execution phase continues after formal training is complete. When workers return to their jobs, managers and supervisors should be prompted to check in with their direct reports to ask how the training went, what they learned, and how they will apply it on the job. Specific goals, if not defined prior to training, should be documented, and progress checked regularly. Since many managers and supervisors may be too busy, consider setting up a system in which peers encourage and hold each other accountable for performance.

At this point, the training team should be keeping a finger on the pulse of what is happening in the on-the-job environment through communication with managers and supervisors, and perhaps a handful of training graduates. Data should be collected and analyzed to see if the program is on track to meet targeted goals.

Success factors and instances of success should be analyzed to determine if there is a way to propagate them across the initiative. Barriers to success and areas where training graduates are not performing to standard should be identified, analyzed for root causes, and resolved. Instead of sweeping performance problems or outcome shortfalls under the rug, embrace them as opportunities to reconnect with managers, participants, and stakeholders to talk about what is going on and how to get the program reengaged.

Progress reports should be provided to training graduates, their supervisors and managers, and senior leadership to reassure them that progress is being made and to enlist their support when needed.

During implementation, plan modifications are to be expected and should be welcomed as opportunities to keep programs on track and ensure that they produce the intended results. Continuous improvement requires continuous evaluation. Instead of simply measuring and reporting what happened after the initiative is complete, maximize program outcomes and your own contribution by continually reporting and positively influencing what happens along the way.

Demonstration of Value Phase

When a program has continued for long enough that an appreciable amount of data has been gathered related to on-the-job application and organizational results, you can begin to compile the first of several interim reports, or the final report, to formally share the program progress and outcomes. The types of information to include in these reports are outlined in chapter 15.

Training value can be reported using a variety of methods, including a dashboard, a verbal presentation supported by graphics or, least favorably, a written or narrative report. Think of it this way: if you were the prosecuting attorney making your case, would you hand the judge and jury a lengthy written report with no illustrations? Or would you tell a compelling story, with great emotion in your voice, and support it with large, color illustrations and an assortment of credible witnesses? The latter is what wins cases, and it is also what effectively demonstrates program value. Do all you can to get the opportunity to tell your story of value to stakeholders in person, even if it's just for a few minutes.

The demonstration of value phase is actually the shortest and most straightforward because you are simply compiling the planned data and telling the story of value. It is only so simple, however, if a good plan was created and followed in the first place.

It would be fair to say that many training professionals today do not start with a defined plan. After training, they reach this phase and then try to work backwards to evaluate value that may or may not have been created in the first place and was not systematically supported and monitored along the way. This unfortunate situation cannot really be resolved in arrears; an effective plan to create and demonstrate program value needs to exist from the start.

Training Is Like Flying a Plane

Think of training like flying a plane. Would a pilot take off without first inspecting the plane, reviewing the flight plan, and making a note of the destination? Probably not. The pilot needs to ensure that the plane is in good repair and has enough fuel to make it to the final destination.

When taking off, would the pilot turn off the radar, shut down the instrument panel, and silence the radio while in flight? Of course not. Without radar, the pilot wouldn't be able to detect any threats; without the instruments, there would be no way to know how the plane is functioning; and without the radio, there would be no communication about issues, problems, or flight plans. The pilot could look out the window but would not have enough scope of vision to keep the plane safe. Ultimately, the pilot would be flying blind.

Conducting training without performing the steps in the planning and execution phases of a program is just like flying blind. If you fail to identify the destination and flight plan during the planning phase, it is unlikely that you will arrive there, or at least not very efficiently. If you do not consider the resources you have available and resolve any preexisting conditions, the program could be ineffective.

If you do not monitor what is happening during the critical on-the-job application period following training, you have no idea what, if any, progress is being made toward the goal. It sounds like a total waste of time and resources to "train blind," but it happens every day. Make sure that every mission-critical initiative begins with a plan for what will happen before, during, and after training to make the intended impact on the desired outcomes.

Summary

It is important to develop an effective evaluation strategy. Properly executed training with good Level 1 scores typically leads to significant Level 2 Learning; good Level 3 application predictably delivers good Level 4 business results. The problem the L&D industry seems to ignore is that there is almost no predictive evidence that good Level 2 leads to significant Level 3. This is often referred to as the great divide. For L&D professionals and functions to be a future force, they must find a way to bridge that divide. It means finding ways to connect L&D with the business using pre-training, training, post-training, and purposeful evaluation.

Training programs are not all created equal. Thus, robust evaluation efforts should focus on those that most likely will positively contribute to mission and business success. This is best accomplished by working through three phases: planning, execution, and demonstration of value. Planning involves conversations with stakeholders and other internal partners to determine criteria for Level 4 success, performance needs to create those successes, and training to prepare employees to perform their jobs better.

Planning begins with Level 4, then moves down to Level 3 and, then and only then, to Levels 2 and 1. Execution involves all learning activities leveraged by post-training support and accountability. Demonstrating training's ultimate business impact is best done by blending quantitative and qualitative data in the form of a story of value, powerfully presented to stakeholders.

CHAPTER 4

The Kirkpatrick
Foundational Principles

Because the Kirkpatrick Model has developed organically over more than 55 years, there are many cases of misuse and misinterpretation. The Kirkpatrick Foundational Principles illustrate the meaning that Don Kirkpatrick intended when he published his first works on the four levels in 1959.

Kirkpatrick Foundational Principles

1. The end is the beginning.
2. Return on expectations (ROE) is the ultimate indicator of value.
3. Business partnership is necessary to bring about positive ROE.
4. Value must be created before it can be demonstrated.
5. A compelling chain of evidence demonstrates your bottom-line value.

Kirkpatrick Foundational Principle #1:
The End Is the Beginning

Effective training and development begins before the program even starts. Don Kirkpatrick said it best in his book *Evaluating Training Programs: The Four Levels*:

Trainers must begin with desired results (Level 4) and then determine what behavior (Level 3) is needed to accomplish them. Then trainers must determine the attitudes, knowledge, and skills (Level 2) that are necessary to bring about the desired behavior(s). The final challenge is to present the training program

Start w/ the end in mind

*in a way that enables the participants not only to learn what they need to know
but also to react favorably to the program (Level 1).*

It is important that the results are at the organizational level and are defined in measurable terms so that all involved can see the ultimate destination of the initiative. Clearly defined results will increase the likelihood that resources will be most effectively and efficiently used to accomplish the mission.

Attempting to apply the four levels after an initiative has been developed and delivered makes it difficult, if not impossible, to create significant training value. All four levels must be considered at every step in the program's design, execution, and measurement.

Kirkpatrick Foundational Principle #2: ROE Is the Ultimate Indicator of Value

When executives ask for new training, many learning professionals retreat to their departments and begin designing and developing suitable programs. While a cursory needs assessment may be conducted, it rarely extends to an understanding of the training's contribution to on-the-job performance and Level 4 Results.

Stakeholder expectations define the value that training professionals are responsible for delivering. Learning professionals must ask the stakeholders questions to clarify and refine their expectations on all four Kirkpatrick levels, from leading indicators to the Level 4 Results.

Determining the leading indicators upon which the success of an initiative will be measured is a negotiation process in which the training professional ensures that the expectations are satisfying to the stakeholder and realistic to achieve with the resources available.

Once stakeholder expectations are clear, learning professionals then need to convert those typically general statements into observable, measurable leading indicators by asking the question, "What will success look like to you?" It may take a series of questions to arrive at the final indicators of program success.

Agreement surrounding leading indicators at the beginning of a project eliminates the need to later attempt to prove the value of the initiative. It is understood from the beginning that if the leading indicator targets are met, the initiative will be viewed as a success.

Kirkpatrick Foundational Principle #3: Business Partnership Is Necessary to Bring About Positive ROE

Training events in and of themselves typically produce about 15 percent on-the-job application. To increase application and therefore program results, additional actions must be taken before and after formal training.

Historically, the role of learning professionals has been to accomplish Levels 1 and 2, or just to complete the training event alone. Not surprisingly, this is where learning professionals spend most of their time.

Producing ROE, however, requires a strong Level 3 execution plan. Therefore, it is critical not only to call upon business partners to help identify what success will look like but also to design a cooperative effort throughout the learning and performance processes to maximize results.

Before training, learning professionals need to partner with supervisors and managers to prepare participants for training. Even more critical is the role of the supervisor or manager after the training. They are the key people who reinforce newly learned knowledge and skills through support and accountability. The degree to which this reinforcement and coaching occurs directly correlates to improved performance and positive outcomes.

Kirkpatrick Foundational Principle #4: Value Must Be Created Before It Can Be Demonstrated

Up to 90 percent of training resources are spent on the design, development, and delivery of training events that yield the previously mentioned 15 percent on-the-job application. Reinforcement that occurs after the training event produces the highest level of learning effectiveness, followed by activities that occur before the learning event, yet each typically garners only 5 percent of the training time and budget.

Currently, learning professionals are putting most of their resources into the part of the training process that produces the lowest level of business or organizational results. They are spending relatively little time in the pre-training and follow-up activities that translate into the positive behavior change and subsequent results (Levels 3 and 4) that organizations seek.

Formal training is the foundation of performance and results. To create ultimate value and ROE, however, strong attention must be given to Level 3 activities.

To create maximum value within their organizations, learning professionals must redefine their roles and extend their expertise, involvement, and influence into Levels 3 and 4.

Kirkpatrick Foundational Principle #5: A Compelling Chain of Evidence Demonstrates Your Bottom-Line Value

The training industry is on trial, accused by business leaders of consuming resources in excess of the value delivered to the organization.

Following the Kirkpatrick Foundational Principles and using the Kirkpatrick Model will create a chain of evidence for learning professionals that demonstrates the organizational value of the entire initiative. It consists of quantitative and qualitative data that connect the four levels and show the ultimate contribution of learning and reinforcement to the organization.

Chain of Evidence: Quantitative and qualitative data at each of the four levels that collectively demonstrate the value obtained from an initiative

---

The chain of evidence serves to unify the learning and business functions, not to isolate training or set it apart; it demonstrates the organizational value of working as a team to contribute to mission accomplishment.

When developing a chain of evidence, keep in mind that the levels are not causal or sequential, nor are they of equal importance. When presenting your case, focus on what is most important to the stakeholder audience. Generally speaking, data at Levels 3 and 4 are of most interest. Data related to Levels 1 and 2 should be limited unless a detailed report is requested specifically.

Summary

There are five foundational principles—The End Is the Beginning; ROE Is the Ultimate Indicator of Value; Business Partnership Is Necessary to Bring About Positive ROE; Value Must Be Created Before It Can Be Demonstrated; and A Compelling Chain of Evidence Demonstrates Your Bottom-Line Value. These form the bedrock of the Kirkpatrick Model and together lead to enhanced ROE. These are the key beliefs underpinning Kirkpatrick training evaluation.

Data Collection Guidelines, Methods, and Tools

Part 2 contains guidelines, methods, and tools for gathering program data so that meaningful analysis can be performed. These methods are practical and flexible, so they can be adapted to effectively evaluate any type of program in any organization. We are often asked if they work in education, government, military, and not-for-profit the same way they work in corporations. The answer is yes; they work for any type of organization and any type of program.

We are also asked if the four levels work to evaluate the effectiveness of programs and events other than training programs. The answer to this question is also yes; they can be adapted to evaluate any type of program. For example, the four levels can be used to plan and evaluate product launches, major initiatives, and goal achievement.

One differentiator of the New World Kirkpatrick Model is that the four levels are not used to simply evaluate what happened; they are used as a means by which to maximize implementation and outcomes, so there are more results to report.

The investment in and importance of the program determines the degree to which each level is evaluated. This section provides guidance in determining how you would go about evaluating different types of initiatives and programs, as well as the resources you might assign to the effort.

Importantly, this section punctuates the fact that the levels are not separate and should not be evaluated in isolation from one another. Within the chapters on each of the levels, key principles are introduced, but the actual evaluation tools are covered in chapter 11.

CHAPTER 5

Evaluating Level 1: Reaction

Level 1 Reaction is the level most familiar to learning professionals and arguably one of the simplest to evaluate; however, this does not necessarily mean that it is being evaluated effectively, or even correctly, in most cases. This chapter explains how to evaluate all three components of Level 1 Reaction—engagement, relevance, and customer satisfaction—while conserving resources for evaluating higher, more important levels.

Level 1: Reaction: The degree to which participants find the training favorable, engaging, and relevant to their jobs

---

Methods, Tools, and Techniques

Level 1 is a place to save resources, not spend them. The key with Level 1 is to quickly and efficiently get the information you need to confirm that the quality of the program and instructor are acceptable.

Formative Evaluation Methods

One simple and inexpensive way to obtain the required information is to incorporate formative evaluation methods into your programs, if you are not using them already. Formative means to evaluate during the program. These are the benefits of using formative methods:

- The trainer gets feedback immediately and can adjust the teaching approach and/or program content to meet learner needs.
- Facilities-related issues, such as room temperature, catering, and lighting, may also be addressed right away, and with few resources.
- Engagement and satisfaction increase because learners are being heard and see immediate response to their concerns.
- Engagement increases if distractions and discomforts are resolved.

Here are examples of formative evaluation methods that can be used instead of, or in addition to, the ubiquitous post-program survey:

- **Instructor observation:** Use your senses to determine the degree to which the class is with you.
- **Pulse check:** Stop the class briefly and just ask how things are going. This can also be done at the beginning or end of a break. Pulse checks can be built into the program design, or can be added if the instructor senses that there is a problem.
- **Dedicated observer:** If a program is new and very important or expensive, it may be worth the investment to have a dedicated observer in the room to watch the class dynamics. If you plan to do this, introduce the observer to the participants and say that he or she is there to observe the instructor.

Summative Evaluation Methods

Summative forms of Level 1 evaluation, particularly surveys, are the most common. Surveys are not bad, but keep in mind that the time that training participants spend completing surveys, trainers spend reviewing survey responses, and someone spends time tabulating the survey results adds up to a lot of expended resources. Focus your post-program survey on the most important elements that you plan to aggregate and monitor over time, and from program to program.

Examples of items to evaluate in a written post-program survey include overall satisfaction with the program, engagement in the program based on how the trainer taught it, relevance of the program material to the participant's job, and general view on the program quality. Specific examples of questions you may ask are provided in chapter 11.

For new and mission-critical programs, consider using interviews and focus groups to get more in-depth information. These methods can also be used if the evaluation form or formative observation raises concerns that you would like to research in more detail.

Timing

Level 1 is most typically measured immediately after the training event because the percentage of evaluation forms returned is likely to be higher. "Holding people hostage" to obtain their completed evaluation form is effective for guaranteeing a high response rate, but consider if it is worth the impact it may have on the quality of responses.

While response rate is an important factor, also keep in mind that participants can provide only limited information in the moments after their training has been completed. The benefit of delaying the Level 1 measurement until later is that people may have a different opinion about the quality of the program after they have attempted to apply the concepts they learned. Waiting a few days or weeks can also neutralize the effect of a highly charismatic instructor and elicit more objective feedback on his or her effectiveness as a facilitator.

Keep in mind as well that new employees and supervisors cannot answer questions about relevance right after the program because they have never done their jobs before and do not know if what they learned will be relevant or not. After several months, it would be good to ask them, "What do you wish you had known up front that would have helped make your new job easier?"

Keep It Simple

You may get to this heading and think, "That's it?!?" Yes, that's it. Level 1 is often overthought and overdone; it's a waste of time and resources that could be put to more benefit at other levels.

Focus on formative evaluation for Level 1. This will allow you to obtain feedback when you can still do something about it if there are corrections that need to be made.

Ask just a few Level 1 questions in your post-program evaluation, which is probably in the form of a survey. Only ask the questions you plan to track and report. Based on the program content, determine if you can gather this information at the end of the program, if you are better off delaying asking these questions until later, or if a blend will get you the best possible information.

Yes, it really IS that simple.

Summary

Level 1 Reaction is the level most familiar to learning professionals, and one of the simplest to evaluate. Focus on formative methods to evaluate the three components of Level 1—engagement, relevance, and customer satisfaction—and conserve resources for evaluating higher, more important levels. Ask just a few questions that you plan to track and report in your post-program evaluation, which most often takes the form of a survey.

CHAPTER 6

Evaluating Level 2: Learning

Level 2 Learning is familiar to most training professionals. As it is largely in the control of the training professional, it is typically evaluated in some way. Level 2 is more often overdone than underdone in terms of resources employed, or perhaps done in isolation from or without consideration of the overall program goal of increasing job performance and maximizing organizational results.

This chapter describes how to evaluate the five components of Level 2 Learning—knowledge, skills, attitude, confidence, and commitment—while conserving resources for evaluating higher, more important levels.

Level 2: Learning: The degree to which participants acquire the intended knowledge, skills, attitude, confidence, and commitment based on their participation in the training

---

Methods, Tools, and Techniques

It is important to be purposeful and deliberate when deciding how and to what degree you evaluate Level 2 to ensure there are enough resources to get across the bridge from training to Levels 3 and 4.

Virtually any activity, discussion, or interaction during a class could be evaluated to assess accomplishment of Level 2. If you select a particular activity as one from which you plan to capture data, consider the minimum acceptable threshold for learning or criteria for success.

Sometimes instructional designers get wrapped up in adding lots of "stuff" to a course—activities, games, themes, or trinkets. Make sure you step back to think about how these experiences will actually contribute to learning and give you the data you need to show that an acceptable level of learning has taken place. The usefulness of the resulting information should be a key consideration when designing learning experiences.

Also think about what information you need to have to be credible to the people who will be judging your performance in terms of the learning of your course participants. What quantitative or qualitative data would they need or want? Contrary to popular belief, most stakeholders are really not interested in Level 2 data. They simply expect that by the time participants leave training, they know what to do.

In Level 2, it is not uncommon to run into some academic snobbery that can be counterproductive to efficient and resource-effective learning. This isn't school anymore; this is real life. If you find yourself spending lots of time structuring multiple types and levels of learning objectives, we are talking to you. Remember that learning is simply a means to an end; we learn so that we can perform our jobs better and ultimately contribute more to our organizations.

Here is a list of common formative methods for evaluating Level 2 Learning:

- knowledge test/check
- discussion
- individual/group activity
- role play
- simulation.

Here is a list of common summative methods for evaluating Level 2 Learning:

- knowledge test/quiz/post-test
- presentation
- teach back: After learning something during the program, participants teach portions of the material to their classmates as a way to confirm their own understanding.
- action planning: At the end of the program, participants create a plan for how they will apply what they learned on the job and what they will accomplish, and then they have regular touch points on their progress.
- demonstration/performance test
- survey
- interview
- focus group/group interview.

Multiple components of Level 2 can be evaluated simultaneously with many of these methods, so do not feel as though you need to address each individually. Ideally, you will create a plan that evaluates all of the components as efficiently as possible as you proceed through the training program, such that at the end, you have confirmed that each has been accomplished and documented satisfactorily.

Evaluating Knowledge

There are not typically many questions about how to evaluate knowledge. It is generally a question of practicality as to what method is used to ascertain if program participants know and understand the content.

Don Kirkpatrick wrote that using pre- and post-tests is a good idea. In the modern business world where things move quickly and resources are stretched, their use is only recommended when required by your stakeholders, when there is a specific business need for the data, or when the program can be modified based on pre-test findings to save resources and increase effectiveness. Also, keep in mind that Don worked for a university. In an academic setting, there is generally more acceptance of and use for testing. Some private-sector organizations do not allow testing, or find it to be culturally undesirable.

The New World approach to evaluating at Level 2 is to incorporate a variety of activities into the training that inherently test participant knowledge. For example, participants can discuss a key concept in a table group and report back key points to the entire class. They would not be able to do this if they did not know the concept. Or, participants can play a game in which the correct responses relate to the key points in the material being taught.

Even if stakeholders do not ask for proof that knowledge was obtained during training, you would be smart to capture it in case you need it. This data can end the "cycle of insanity"—performance is poor, so training is conducted; after training, on-the-job performance and results do not improve, so supervisors say, "Let's send them back to training."

If you find yourself in this situation, it would be helpful to be able to produce data, even if it is simply your own notes and observations from class, to validate that when participants left training, they indeed knew the content. Then, you are in a position to have a productive conversation with the well-meaning supervisor about what might be causing the subpar performance and what will resolve it.

Evaluating Skill

Evaluating skill requires the training participant to actually do or demonstrate something. Seldom can skill level be evaluated with an oral or written test, unless the skill in question is actually something that is completed orally or in writing.

For example, how excited would you be to board a plane with a new pilot who announced over the intercom, "Folks, this is my first time flying this type of aircraft, but I took an online course and got 100 percent on the multiple-choice written test on how to operate it, so we are going to be just fine today."

When there is a skill to be performed, the test should involve performance of the skill in as real an environment as possible, whether simply in the classroom or in some type of simulator. For practical training, such as assembling something, this is pretty straightforward. You want to have the parts that need to be assembled, and an environment where participants actually assemble them.

For what is often referred to as soft-skills training, involving things such as communication, leadership, and interpersonal skills, it is important that during the planning phase you clearly define exactly what training graduates are supposed to DO or SAY on the job. This is your guide for what needs to be simulated and practiced during training.

For example, in new supervisor training, one skill that might be part of the program is providing constructive feedback to a direct report who is not performing up to standard. In this case, you would want to use a real scenario brought to class by a participant, or a realistic example, and have participants actually role play the conversation. The instructor and other participants observe and provide feedback, and participants practice until the consensus is that they said what they are supposed to say.

As mentioned, evaluation of the five components of learning is not mutually exclusive. When you create meaningful activities that help participants to learn concepts and practice new skills at the same time, you are building their positive attitude about doing these things on the job, as well as their confidence and commitment to do them. However, evaluating attitude, confidence, and commitment is a bit different than evaluating knowledge and skill because they are less tangible.

Evaluating Attitude

In the case of participant attitude toward performing the skills being taught, determine if the participants see the benefit in doing what they are being asked to do on the job.

Informally, this might be evaluated by the instructor's observations. For example, are program participants actively involved in training activities and discussions, or are they multi-tasking on their phones? Are they asking questions and offering responses, or simply sitting still in their chairs? Do participants have happy, interested looks on their faces, or are they frowning, scowling, or otherwise looking like they do not enjoy or agree with the program content? Formative evaluation of participant attitudes is an effective way to determine if additional discussion needs to take place around on-the-job performance expectations.

If the training program has come about in part due to something that participants are not doing on the job but should, it may be time to plan a discussion surrounding attitude into the program content.

For example, let's say a hospital has mandated training because healthcare providers are not washing their hands prior to working with a new patient. Logically, the problem is likely not that the providers do not know how to wash their hands; it is more likely that they do not feel like it, do not see the importance, or perhaps do not have convenient access to hand-washing facilities prior to each patient encounter. Ideally, the situation has been fully examined before training, but realistically, as training professionals ourselves, we know that sometimes trainers simply walk into the classroom and have to deal with whatever they get.

In this case, the trainer would be wise to have a discussion with participants, whether planned into the program or not, about reasons why people may not always wash their hands. It serves as a quick confirmation to find out if they know they are supposed to wash their hands before each and every patient encounter. I am about 99 percent positive that they do.

From there, ask a question such as, "What are some of the reasons you have heard that hands don't get washed every time?" This depersonalized question should get the ball rolling for a frank conversation about what is really happening in the workplace, and if there is a problem with attitude or with seeing the importance of hand washing to prevent the spread of disease.

Ideally, the importance of hand washing was addressed prior to the program, as part of the background information provided to participants to increase their engagement. If not, this is a good time to restate the reasons for hand washing. It could also lend itself to a table activity or group discussion in which participants brainstorm the positive outcomes of hand washing and the negative outcomes of skipping it. Coming up with these ideas on their own is a good way to solidify a positive attitude about hand washing, or whatever you are teaching the class to do.

If the nature of the training program is such that attitude about performing the required skills on the job is in question, it also makes sense to include a related item in the post-program evaluation. This way, the observations and notes from the instructor can be supported with anonymous, numeric data showing if the group was generally of the correct or incorrect attitude by the end of the program.

Evaluating Confidence and Commitment

Confidence and commitment to perform new skills on the job are built in part through a good training program that provides ample opportunity to practice, ask questions, and discuss expectations.

Skills that are new or challenging generally require a dedicated discussion or some type of activity during which participants can share any questions or concerns they may have before they return to work and are expected to perform. It is not uncommon to hear participants say as they leave training, "That guy has no idea what we are up against in the field. This is not going to work."

Many training professionals avoid opening up a conversation about application concerns and barriers because it is outside of their comfort zone. Often, training programs are so packed full of content that no time is available to discuss these real-world concerns. However, conducting this type of discussion may be the difference between a botched initiative and one in which barriers to performance are removed, allowing the organization to truly make progress toward its highest goals at record speed.

During discussion surrounding confidence and commitment, training professionals should listen carefully to determine where the stated objections or concerns stem from. Is it something related to knowledge and skill? If so, maybe it can be resolved during the program with additional activities and application, or later with follow-up training.

Or, is the stated concern something in the on-the-job environment, such as a supervisor who provides alternate instructions, lack of resources or tools, conflicting goals, no system of accountability, or lack of support if a person needs help? This information should be documented to report to managers and supervisors.

For soft-skills training or training that is advanced or complicated in nature, including a question or two about confidence and commitment in the post-program evaluation is wise. If participants are shy or unwilling to share their true feelings in a group setting, this can allow you to get a good read as to where the class really is in terms of readiness to perform on the job.

If there are real barriers to application and confidence is therefore low, be aware of the fact that self-reports of commitment, such as creation of an action plan, will not likely be honest.

Until the on-the-job barriers and challenges are cleared, even the most "successful" training program will yield little or no organizational impact, and therefore will not be successful in the eyes of stakeholders. Training professionals can be part of major organizational improvements by candidly bringing forward barriers and participating in a task force to correct them.

The training professional is wise to keep all Level 2 data, even if it is not reported to stakeholders. If the cycle of insanity occurs, in which desired performance has not been achieved and managers request additional training, this data can be pulled out to show that after training, participants knew what they needed to know, demonstrated their skill adequately, could articulate why it is important to do these things on the job, and expressed at least a reasonable level of confidence and commitment to do it. So, if performance is not what was expected, the likely cause is something in the work environment and will not be resolved with another round of the same training.

Timing

Most Level 2 evaluation should be formative in nature. Training programs should be designed around building participant knowledge, skill, attitude, confidence, and commitment, and then include methods to evaluate and capture the required data.

Immediately following the program, it is possible to include questions about all components, with the exception of physical skills, in post-program surveys, interviews, and focus groups. This may be a way to collect numeric data to underpin in-class observations and activity records captured by the facilitator. It can also be a convenient way to document written testimonials.

If you are interested in collecting pre-test and post-test data at Level 2, one easy and efficient way to do it is through a retrospective pre- and post-assessment item. Use this technique after training is complete by asking participants about their level of proficiency before training and their current level of proficiency. The important thing to note is that participants answer both questions after the training, because before training they may not know what they do not know. The retrospective pre- and post-assessment provides data similar to what you would gather using pre-assessments and post-assessments, but with less time and fewer resources. (In chapter 11, questions 6–8 in Table 11-6 provide an example of retrospective pre- and post-assessment items.)

If Level 2 is evaluated completely during the training program, there is really no great need to perform summative evaluation on a delayed basis. However, if observations or data show that participant knowledge, skill, attitude, confidence, or commitment has eroded since training, then a follow-up evaluation could validate if this is the case. Fair warning, though—such problems are not typically related to Level 2; they are more typically tied to on-the-job issues at Level 3.

Summary

Level 2 Learning is familiar to most training professionals, and since it largely rests within their control, is often overdone. Be deliberate and purposeful in determining how you will evaluate the five components of Level 2 Learning—knowledge, skill, attitude, confidence, and commitment.

Level 2 evaluation is primarily formative in nature. Virtually any activity during the program could be used for Level 2 evaluation, if you wish. With the current pressure to complete learning in the minimum amount of time, focus on meeting the threshold for what is required, and keep extra games and activities to a minimum.

The traditional pre-test and post-test approach should only be used if there is a specific use for the data; for example, if you have the ability to modify the program content on the spot to match participant knowledge levels.

CHAPTER 7

Evaluating Level 3: Behavior

Level 3 Behavior is the most important level because training alone will not yield enough organizational results to be viewed as successful. Level 3 is also the most disruptive to traditional training evaluation practices.

Level 3: Behavior: The degree to which participants apply what they learned during training when they are back on the job

---

It is shocking that even for mission-critical programs there is often no clarity on what people are supposed to do on the job as a result of the training. There is also seldom an adequate plan to assist people in performing the critical behaviors and holding them accountable.

Level 3 is more than just evaluating; it is a comprehensive, continuous performance monitoring and improvement system. The degree to which required drivers are identified and implemented is one of the most important parts of a successful plan. Level 3 is a challenging level that for decades has appeared to be a "no-man's land." L&D has shied away from taking their share of responsibility for it, and organizations are ultimately focused on Level 4 Results. Level 3 truly is the missing link in moving from learning to results.

Research on the Importance of Post-Training Support

Here's why drivers are so important. Dr. Robert O. Brinkerhoff, a professor emeritus at Western Michigan University and an authority on training evaluation, has for decades studied the factors that lead to on-the-job application. He conducted a study in 2006 that had two groups. The first group used a traditional training approach focused on the design, development, and delivery of the training event. They invested very little in pre-training preparation or post-training follow-up and support.

After training, 15 percent of the training graduates never bothered to try to perform the new behaviors they learned in training. Seventy percent of them tried but failed due to a variety of factors in the job environment, such as differing methods being required by their manager, discomfort in performing the new skill, or not having the necessary equipment or tools. Sometimes they just did not see a reason to put forth the effort to try something new, and there was no punishment for continuing to do what had always been done. Only 15 percent of the training graduates in this group managed to sustain new behaviors on the job.

The second group in the study, which was more difficult to find, used a different approach. They invested a quarter of their time talking with business leaders to identify targeted Level 4 outcomes, preparing training participants and their supervisors for what would happen during training and discussing their roles before, during, and after training. They invested another quarter of their resources in the training event itself. They reserved half of their resources to support performance of critical behaviors on the job, or in other words, employing their required drivers.

The results for the second group were dramatically different than the first: only 5 percent of the training graduates never bothered to try the new skills. Only 10 percent tried but failed due to reasons in their on-the-job environment. A full 85 percent of the training graduates were successful in sustaining the new behaviors on the job.

Keep in mind that the second group had exactly the same resources as the first group; they just used them differently. In our opinion, the 15 percent application accomplished by the first group is not going to bring about any significant Level 4 Results. Therefore, what this research means from the Kirkpatrick perspective is that training professionals have to concern themselves with more than training programs; they need to get involved in the on-the-job environment. Resources must be reallocated from traditional training programs to a blended learning approach (Figure 7-1).

Defining the Few, Critical Behaviors

Before Level 3 can be evaluated, it needs to be defined. This critical step is missed in many programs. Identify the few, critical behaviors that will most influence Level 4: Results and establish them as the path from learning to desired outcomes.

Take this example. Jim reviewed an award-winning corporate onboarding program for one of his clients. He was troubled by the fact that he did not see defined performance expectations for the new hires when they emerged from this week-long

Figure 7-1. Differences in Training Outcomes

GROUP 1 - TRADITIONAL APPROACH

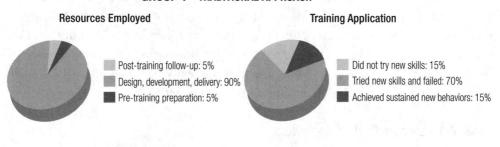

Resources Employed

Post-training follow-up: 5%
Design, development, delivery: 90%
Pre-training preparation: 5%

Training Application

Did not try new skills: 15%
Tried new skills and failed: 70%
Achieved sustained new behaviors: 15%

GROUP 2 - LEARNING AND PERFORMANCE APPROACH

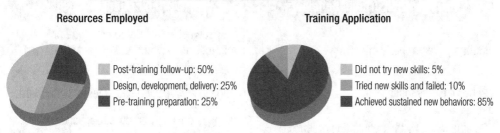

Resources Employed

Post-training follow-up: 50%
Design, development, delivery: 25%
Pre-training preparation: 25%

Training Application

Did not try new skills: 5%
Tried new skills and failed: 10%
Achieved sustained new behaviors: 85%

Telling Training's Story, *Rob Brinkerhoff, 2006*

immersion program. He asked them to add one Likert scale item to their post-program evaluation: I am clear about what is expected of me when I get back to my job.

The client piloted the question for the next few sessions, and the score was significantly lower than for all other items in the survey. As a result, they redesigned and renamed the program to focus more on performance, rather than just awareness and acclimation.

There are numerous behaviors that people can and do perform on the job. What makes them critical is that if they are performed reliably, they will have the biggest impact on the targeted program outcomes. The key word with these behaviors is *few*.

Too many behaviors also confuse employees as to what will truly positively affect their careers and their contributions to the organization. Finally, too many behaviors make for a totally unmanageable support system.

The first step in defining critical behaviors is to work with supervisors, line managers, and perhaps a group of high performers to discuss what behaviors they believe would bring about the desired outcomes previously negotiated with stakeholders.

Critical behaviors need to be specific, observable, and measurable. They need to pass what we call the "video test," which means that one can actually capture them on camera and be able to explain what is happening. One also needs to be able to count the number of times a particular behavior occurs, and even better, note the quality or accuracy of the performed behavior.

Critical behaviors should be defined in terms that connect them to the outcome (Table 7-1). It's common to see critical behaviors phrased as "Leaders should manage their direct reports effectively." Unfortunately, this does not pass the video test, and it is not specific. This would be a better critical behavior: "Leaders will conduct weekly team meetings that include all direct reports to document project status and required actions." An observer can confidently report if the team leader conducted a weekly meeting and documented project status and required actions.

Table 7-1. Sample Critical Behaviors

Poorly written critical behaviors	Well-written critical behaviors
Manage direct reports effectively.	Conduct weekly team meetings that include all direct reports to document project status and required actions.
Perform safety testing.	Complete all specified safety tests to standard.
Be able to follow the negotiation process.	Use the negotiation process to resolve all intradepartmental conflicts.

Once the critical behaviors are defined, the threshold of acceptable performance levels should be determined. By definition, well-written critical behaviors require 100 percent compliance. However, it is wise to address the reality in the actual job environment, and what will occur if compliance is less than 100 percent. If a behavior is termed critical but it is acceptable to not perform it regularly, then it is not truly critical.

Keep in mind that critical behaviors are those behaviors performed by the primary training audience. Behaviors performed by or resulting from others are likely required drivers or leading indicators; for example, when a supervisor observes a direct report on the job and provides feedback, that is a required driver. When the direct report does well and a customer is satisfied as a result of that performance, that is a leading indicator.

A Few Words About Competencies

Competency-based organizations have a bit of work to do here. How organizations define competencies varies, but for purposes of this discussion, the concern is with competencies that define skills and traits. By definition, these reside in Level 2, and if the organization wants to keep them, they should be checked for alignment with identified critical behaviors. Organizations tend to want to lead with competencies; however, it is more effective to lead with critical behaviors and select competencies that support them.

For example, if a leadership competency is creating a culture of teamwork, it would need to be defined by critical behaviors such as conducting team meetings at least once per week.

If an organization is insistent about retaining competencies, it is important to ensure that they start with desired business results, consider what performance is required to achieve them, and then think about the required competencies. Leading with competencies is like leading with Level 2 Learning; it is backwards and ineffective.

Methods, Tools, and Techniques

Success at Level 3 is the key to Level 4 Results, so extra attention is given to Level 3 through required drivers, which are processes and systems that reinforce, monitor, encourage, and reward performance of critical behaviors on the job (Table 7-2).

Table 7-2. Required Drivers

SUPPORT	
Reinforce	**Encourage**
Follow-up modules	Coaching
Work review checklist	Mentoring
On-the-job training (OJT)	
Self-directed learning	**Reward**
Refreshers	Recognition
Job aids	Pay for performance
Reminders	
Executive modeling	
Communities of practice	

ACCOUNTABILITY	
Monitor	
Action learning	Action plan monitoring
Interviews	Dashboard
Observation	Work review
Self-monitoring	Survey
KPIs (key performance indicators)	Touch bases / meetings

Required drivers fall under two headings: support and accountability. Remember the first group in Brinkerhoff's study, where 70 percent of the training graduates tried to do the right thing on the job but failed for some reason? Support tools are for them. For the 15 percent who didn't even try, there are accountability methods. As a package, support and accountability are helpful for everyone.

Many drivers are performed by the managers and supervisors on the job, who are with the training graduates every day. Some drivers can be performed or supported by training professionals, such as follow-up modules, refreshers, job aids, and reminders. Some drivers relate to company policy and human resources, and may also involve other departments. Training graduates themselves and their peers can also perform some of their own required drivers.

For mission-critical programs, make sure you have a solid plan for monitoring both compliance with critical behaviors and progress toward desired results. Also, create a support plan with at least one item from the reinforcing, encouraging, and rewarding categories. Keep in mind that drivers often already exist and simply need to be aligned to key programs. Be realistic about what will likely be effective, as well as possible, within your organization.

Methods of Monitoring

If there is no system of accountability in place after training, even those with good intentions will give up or wander back to the way they are used to doing things. People are conditioned by the fact that organizations monitor and report on what they think is important, such as sales, profitability, customer retention, employee turnover, defective rate, scrap or waste, and market share, for example.

If something is measured, it means it is important. While it may not truly follow, this gives the impression that what is not measured is not important. For this reason, one or more methods of accountability must be put in place for important initiatives and non-negotiable behaviors.

The most common method of post-program monitoring is a 90-day survey. The concern about this is that for 89 days, there was probably no accountability. So, if you are inclined to use a survey to gather data, understand that this is a very incomplete and cursory approach to monitoring performance. Realize that sending a 90-day survey after every program probably just desensitizes people to them and "surveys people out."

Better methods of monitoring performance include observation and work review. These can be performed by a supervisor, training professional, or even a peer. Accountability does not need to be solely assigned to the manager or supervisor, who is probably already overburdened.

Recognizing the general lack of resources for monitoring, consider including a method of self-accountability in the program, such as weekly reports or performance checklists that are submitted by the training graduate to a supervisor or someone else who will review them regularly.

Methods of Reinforcing

The first group of required drivers in the support category consists of methods of reinforcing. These are items that remind training graduates of what they are supposed to do and provide additional training and guidance, if needed.

Many of these reinforcing methods can be designed and built in advance of training, such as job aids, reminders, refreshers, and on-the-job training modules. Reinforcing is a category in which training likely performs the key role.

In the reinforcing category, technology can actually be a plus and feel more personal than one would expect. For example, after our own programs, we have a series of follow-up messages that can be scheduled to launch automatically via email once per week. In these messages, we reference what graduates might want to consider at that time, give them links to more information, and invite them to contact us with questions or comments. Often, participants view these as personal messages from us and take them as opportunities to reconnect with us.

Methods of Encouraging

Encouragement probably occurs on the job all the time, but plan ways for it to occur a bit more formally and regularly in support of the identified critical behaviors.

For complex or largely new critical behaviors, such as those of a new supervisor, a formal coach or mentor could be assigned. Obviously, this is only practical in situations in which the critical behavior package is important to organizational success and complicated enough that the training graduate may struggle to perform it well.

Managers and supervisors have multiple preexisting priorities, so there is a movement toward more peer mentoring and encouragement programs.

Methods of Rewarding

As it relates to training and performance, a broad view of the concept of rewards is often beneficial so you are not beholden to the financial realities of a volatile economy or budget.

On the formal and extrinsic level, obtain confirmation from managers and perhaps human resources during the program design phase that existing reward systems are compatible with what training graduates will be asked to do on the job.

For example, you would not want to train sales professionals to follow a set call schedule and a sales call outline, but then allow them to earn a bonus even if they do not adhere to the schedule and the script. Doing so sends an overall message that the critical behaviors are not critical at all; they are optional.

On an informal or intrinsic level, training can work with managers and supervisors to create equally important rewards for those who perform the critical behaviors reliably, and disincentives for those who do not. Here are some examples:

- a departmental "jeans day"
- small prizes, such as movie tickets and coupons for favorite coffee shops and lunch locations
- early dismissal Fridays
- recognition in the company newspaper, bulletin board, intranet, or website
- fun trophies, plaques, or awards that circulate on a daily, weekly, or monthly basis.

Sometimes just having someone notice and mention good performance is even more meaningful than any particular tangible reward. For example, a manager from another department could say, "Charlie, I noticed that you stayed late last week to get the order packed and shipped on time. I really appreciate it, and the customer has already called to thank us for our prompt service."

Required Drivers Are Not Mutually Exclusive

The four types of required drivers are not mutually exclusive; a weekly team meeting could address all four dimensions:

1. **Monitoring:** If each team member knows that individual or team performance will be reviewed during the meeting, then they know it will be uncomfortable if they have not done what was required.
2. **Reinforcing:** Having performance reporting on the meeting agenda stresses its importance.
3. **Encouraging:** Supervisors and team members can encourage each other by listening to challenges and assisting in resolving them.
4. **Rewarding:** Employees with good performance can receive recognition and rewards during the meeting.

Required Drivers Are an Integrated Package

The required driver package is critical to success, yet viewed as the most complicated to execute; therefore, it is time well spent to discuss what will be both practical and feasible within your organization. Designing a package that includes elements that will not be supported or that are out of the comfort zone of those who need to perform them will likely not be effective.

It is not uncommon for people to voice this objection: "Our resources are limited. There is no way we can do this." To address this valid concern, we offer the example of our own company, which has only three full-time employees besides ourselves.

Each employee has a set of critical behaviors that are connected to various leading indicators for the success of the company.

Tasks that occur regularly as part of Kirkpatrick events have written procedures that all employees follow. We use an online task management system in which each person has all of his or her daily tasks entered. Employees also track their work time there, so at any point, any employee can see if another employee has completed a given task, or what they have done that day, or any day. We, as the owners, review this daily, or anytime we like. This provides the opportunity to provide encouragement or constructive criticism based on what we see.

At the beginning of each week, each team member reviews his or her assigned tasks for the upcoming week and actually plots them into the calendar. In this way, they can see if they can complete all required work within their working hours. This not only creates a plan for the week that is shared with the team but also provides the opportunity to head off bottlenecks, reassign tasks, or add resources if needed.

There is a daily team meeting during which current and future projects are discussed, and every team member is invited to add items to the agenda for discussion. Completed programs are formally reviewed as a way to identify best practices and areas of weakness.

Each employee has a supervisor touch base one or more days per week to discuss current workload and get any questions answered. There is also a more formal monthly performance appraisal in which performance is discussed more globally.

Wendy performs most of the traditional supervisory responsibilities, including checking for task completion and quality, and ensuring that processes are followed. Jim serves as a performance coach, encouraging and recognizing good behavior, and working with those who need some improvement.

We hold ourselves accountable to these same guidelines; we make and share our calendars, track our time, lead all team meetings, and touch bases. There is total transparency; there is nowhere to hide. Executing Kirkpatrick programs with excellence is mission critical, so these things are nonnegotiable.

Common Objections to Implementing a Driver Package

Here are the most common objections from training professionals related to their role in driving performance and results, and our responses:

1. It Is Too Time Consuming

If you or your organization is of the belief that it is too time consuming to make sure that performance occurs and desired results are obtained, then you may have not defined critical behaviors properly. If the behaviors are truly mission critical for your success, you cannot afford subpar performance or results. However, if the behaviors are truly not mission critical, then save the resources there and have them available for those that are.

2. I Cannot Access the Training Graduates

With all due respect, this is simply an excuse. In today's age of easy electronic access, even those on top-secret military missions are connected electronically at least sometimes. Ongoing access to participants is a key item to negotiate prior to a program, and you need to insist on the importance of it for the success of the program.

At Kirkpatrick Partners, every person we train is outside of our organization, and therefore not simple for us to contact. We count on the relationships we build during our programs to earn the right to stay in touch with people; we require full contact information from participants up front, and we build post-program support and accountability into our programs. If we can do it, so can you.

3. I Cannot Get Access to Performance and Outcome Data

This is a real issue that often requires extra effort and discussion. During program planning, the ability to access the required data, or cleansed versions of it, needs to be negotiated. When Wendy was a corporate training manager, it took about six months for her manager to obtain the necessary permissions for her to see sales reports so that she could correlate training to performance to results on an individual basis.

Find an advocate who will help you to get the data you require.

4. I Cannot Control What Happens After People Leave Training

It is true that training professionals typically have little or no control over what happens after training. Training graduates often leave and might even go to another part of the country, or world, to resume their work. Instead of worrying about controlling training graduate behavior, part of your training and follow-up plan needs to include the means to influence it; this is, in a nutshell, the required driver package.

The role of training is the "Monitor and Adjust" box in the New World Kirkpatrick Model (Figure 2-1); monitor the performance of critical behaviors and required drivers, even if from afar, and make sure that the program is on track to deliver the desired outcomes. Stay involved by reporting the status to stakeholders and participate in discussions when there are barriers.

Timing

Don Kirkpatrick originally taught that behavior should be measured before training as a baseline, and then afterwards to see the change. If you have the resources to do this and your stakeholders want to see this data, then great.

For most businesses, however, it is more practical to just focus on evaluating performance of the critical behaviors after training. After all, there probably would not have been a call for training if behavior was acceptable.

When evaluating behavior, consider when it would be reasonable to start assessing performance, and how often and for how long it should continue to sustain satisfactory levels.

For example, the day after a well-known security breach at Heathrow Airport a number of years ago, U.S. Transportation Security Administration (TSA) agents were carefully monitored to ensure that they identified and removed all liquids and gels in passenger carry-on bags. This type of security issue is straightforward and time sensitive, so 100 percent accountability started immediately and then tapered down to a normal monitoring schedule over time.

If you are teaching communication skills, however, it can be counterproductive to measure progress immediately following the training because people need to practice the new behaviors to get comfortable. Also, the delayed measurement may need to continue for a period of time because it will take longer for people to truly adopt the new behaviors.

Conversely, reinforcement and encouragement should almost always start immediately after training, so make sure your supporting drivers are activated right away. Keep reminding training graduates of the importance of performing the new behaviors. Then, when reasonable, begin monitoring and reporting on the actual performance.

Informal rewards can begin immediately, as you see good performance occurring. Formal rewards, by nature, might be delayed until preliminary outcomes begin to occur.

Summary

Level 3 Behavior is the most important level because training alone will not yield enough organizational results to be viewed as successful. Even for mission-critical programs there is often no clarity on what people are supposed to do on the job as a result of the training. There is also seldom an adequate plan to assist people in performing the critical behaviors and hold them accountable.

Level 3 is more than just evaluating; it is a comprehensive, continuous performance monitoring and improvement system. A required driver package—methods and systems of monitoring, reinforcing, encouraging, and rewarding performance of critical behaviors on the job—needs to be created and implemented.

Level 3 is a challenging level that for decades has appeared to be a "no-man's land." L&D has shied away from taking their share of responsibility for it, and organizations are ultimately focused on Level 4 Results. However, the degree to which Level 3 is implemented is one of the most important parts of a successful plan. Level 3 truly is the missing link in moving from learning to results.

CHAPTER 8

Evaluating Level 4: Results

Level 4 Results is the reason that training is performed. Training's job is not done until its contribution to business results can be demonstrated to and is acknowledged by stakeholders. Sadly, the majority of training professionals don't know how to do this. A percentage of them also stubbornly insist they do not need to do this; they believe their role is simply to impart knowledge.

Simply stated, connecting training to performance to results is not optional for mission-critical programs. This necessitates knowing the organization's true Level 4 result and the key leading indicators.

Level 4: Results: The degree to which targeted outcomes occur as a result of the training and the support and accountability package

Leading Indicators: Short-term observations and measurements that suggest that critical behaviors are on track to create a positive impact on the desired results

Identifying Leading Indicators

Leading indicators provide personalized targets that all contribute to organizational results. They also establish a connection between performance of critical behaviors and the organization's highest-level result. We sometimes call the organizational result the flag at the top of the mountain. Leading indicators are the little flags marching up the mountain toward the desired results at the top, showing progress toward the goal (Figure 8-1).

Figure 8-1. Flags up the Mountain

© *Mark Hatfield*

The first plateau in the lower left corner represents the accomplishment of Levels 1 and 2. This is "base camp," where all is well, and people are prepared, competent, and equipped for the climb. But it is not the summit. It is not even close, and many perils and challenges must be faced to achieve the mountain summit, and business success.

The best way to work with leading indicators is to picture and present them moving up the slope in the order in which they will most likely occur. Each flag indicates a different leading indicator along the path to organizational results.

Here are some common examples of leading indicators (Table 8-1).

Leading indicators sometimes are actually measurements of undesirable situations that did not occur; for example, a "close call," such as stopping a malfunctioning machine before it injures a worker, thwarting a terrorist attack, cleaning up a spill before someone falls, or spotting an error in a spreadsheet before a price is miscalculated.

Table 8-1. Leading Indicators

INTERNAL	
Individual, team, departmental, and/or organizational outcomes	

Quality
- Quality ratings
- Errors
- KPI (key performance indicator) accomplishment

Cost
- Unit product line profitability cost
- Waste / scrap
- Inventory turn rate / cost
- Overhead costs

Volume / Production
- Production rate / output
- First-call customer service resolutions
- Completed projects / initiatives

Efficiency
- Average processing time
- Speed to proficiency
- Speed to market

Compliance
- Audit findings
- External audit findings
- Known incident reports

Employee Satisfaction
- Employee engagement
- Employee satisfaction
- Internal promotions
- Regrettable turnover
- Re-enlistment rate
- Employee job confidence
- Employee initiative

Safety
- Lost-time injuries
- "Close calls"
- Critical incidents

EXTERNAL	
Customer, client, market, and/or industry response	

Customer Response
- Sales volume
- New customers
- Customer call-center usage
- Customer attrition
- Program participation

Market / Industry Response
- External awards and recognition
- External "buzz"
- Brand perception
- Lawsuits and claims
- Press commentary

Customer Satisfaction
- Customer ratings
- Repeat sales
- Unsolicited referrals
- Compliment-to-complaint ratio

Balance of Quantitative and Qualitative Measurements

There are two distinct types of leading indicators, both of which can manifest quantitatively or qualitatively. Internal leading indicators, as you may guess from the name, arise from within an organization and are typically the first to appear. These are things such as production output, quality, sales, employee retention, and the like.

External leading indicators relate to how the customer, client, or benefactor is responding to the critical behaviors that the vendor, supplier, or contractor has performed. These include things such as customer retention, brand recognition, goodwill, and sales from referrals.

When you start to think about your own organization and programs, keep in mind that key outcomes for your department, group, or programs are leading indicators, all of which contribute to the one Level 4 result for the entire organization. This is sometimes difficult for people to understand or accept.

For example, an IT department could have goals of reducing technology costs and averting security breaches. These are leading indicators that can affect the highest-level company results, but they are not the result in and of themselves. The true Level 4 result is likely something such as profitably providing whatever product or service the company offers to the marketplace.

The Benefits of Identifying Leading Indicators

Identifying and leveraging leading indicators is extremely powerful. Here are the benefits of using them.

First, they keep your initiatives on track by serving as the last line of defense against possible failure at Level 4. Monitoring leading indicators along the way gives you time to identify barriers to success and apply the proper interventions before ultimate outcomes are jeopardized.

Second, they serve to reassure your stakeholders by providing interim updates. Reporting the status of leading indicators monthly or even weekly buys time for ultimate results to occur.

Leading indicators act as motivators for training graduates that reduce the dependence on external required drivers. This ultimately saves time and money, with the collateral benefit of increased morale.

Finally, leading indicators provide important data connecting training, on-the-job performance, and the highest-level result.

Methods, Tools, and Techniques

In the past, many people assumed that all Level 4 evaluation was summative. But the introduction of leading indicators creates the opportunity for formative measures.

The first step in preparing to evaluate leading indicators is to define which data you can simply borrow, and which data you will build the tools to gather.

Because Level 4 Results are critically important to the organization, someone is likely already measuring them. Borrowed business and human resources metrics are a common source of data. The key to obtaining this data is building relationships with the people who can provide you with the information you need to evaluate the success of your training, rather than attempting to gather this data yourself.

For example, most for-profit companies have sales, profitability, and increase in market share and growth among their highest-level goals. The sales department is already measuring sales, accounting is tracking profitability, and marketing is probably tracking market share and growth.

Government, military, and not-for-profit organizations typically have a mission they are charged with accomplishing. Often, the mission is less concrete and measurable than the goals of a for-profit organization. In this case, it is important to identify specific metrics that will define if the organization is successful or not in accomplishing its goal.

After determining what data are already available and what might meet your needs, you then can define what tools you may need to build. Typical examples of tools that may need to be built are surveys and a structured question set for interviews and focus groups.

A customer survey is a commonly used tool that may or may not already exist in your organization. The assumption is that happier customers will buy more from you and increase your business through positive word of mouth.

Requests for validation are another way to obtain meaningful numbers or correlate them to training when you don't have direct access to data. Don't be afraid to ask training participants and their managers for their personal testimonials. These requests, either verbally or via email, ask participants to explain how the training has helped them to perform on the job, and the subsequent results. This can make "soft" data more quantifiable (Figure 8-2).

Note that the sample request for validation includes a historical comparison, in which the training graduate or manager is asked to compare his or her performance and results before and after the program. This type of testimonial is usually very powerful to stakeholders because it implies causality: I went to training and implemented new ideas on the job, and then my performance and results improved.

Action planning during training is a good way to set the stage for performance on the job and watching for subsequent results. If you use this method, ensure that training graduates define the outcomes they expect if they perform the critical behaviors.

As you monitor performance and results, you may discover unexpected collateral benefits. For example, if leaders hold cross-functional weekly meetings and work

Figure 8-2. Sample Validation Letter

Dear Colleague,

Your sales team completed a course entitled "Trusted Advisor Sales Excellence" about nine months ago. We in Human Resources are interested in determining the relative value of that training.

Please take five minutes to answer the following questions:

1. Have you seen any change in key sales results over the past nine months? If so, please provide specific details.

2. Are you able to attribute any of that change to the sales training and subsequent follow-up that your team experienced? If so, do you have any evidence to support your conclusion? Please provide any such evidence.

3. Would you be willing to talk with me further about these past months?

Thank you very much for your time and input.

Best Regards,

Betty Van Campen
Human Resources

---

together on major initiatives, the result may not only be higher profitability through collaboration, but also increased employee morale, reduced turnover, and reduced scrap.

Timing

In most cases, it is not reasonable to measure the highest Level 4 result the day after training. However, you may be able to begin monitoring leading indicators much more quickly. Look at each and determine a good start time and interval.

Here is a sports analogy that sums up the timing of Level 4 evaluation: You don't train a football team at the beginning of the season, play all the games and then, at the end of the season, see if you won the Super Bowl. Instead, you track what is working during each game, focusing on making ongoing adjustments to win as many games as possible, get to the playoffs, and continue your "winning ways" to the Super Bowl.

As with evaluating all other levels, evaluating Level 4 is a process, not an event.

Summary

Level 4 Results is the reason that training is performed. Training's job is not done until its contribution to business results can be demonstrated to and is acknowledged by stakeholders. Simply stated, connecting training to performance to results is not optional for mission-critical programs.

Training must be clear on the true Level 4 result for the organization. From there, leading indicators, or short-term observations and measurements that suggest that critical behaviors are on track to create a positive impact on the desired results, should be identified and tracked. Since the true Level 4 result can take time to manifest, leading indicators help to keep initiatives on track, motivate training graduates, and reassure stakeholders that the program is contributing to key organizational outcomes.

CHAPTER 9

Evaluating Beyond Traditional Classroom Training

A frequently asked question about the Kirkpatrick Model is whether it can be used outside of formal classroom training. In this chapter, we explore, with the assistance of three experts in the field, specifically how to apply the New World Kirkpatrick Model to e-learning, informal learning, mobile learning (m-learning), and social learning.

Due to the flexibility of the Kirkpatrick Model, it can be adapted to evaluate any type of learning situation. You simply determine which levels are appropriate to evaluate and select the tools that work in the given situation.

How to Evaluate E-Learning

By William Horton

How well can an evaluation framework conceived in the 1950s apply to 21st-century e-learning and its variants? Back then, computers weighed tons, and the term *network* referred to television stations. Yet, that four-level framework still applies quite well.

Like all effective engineering models, the Kirkpatrick Model concerns itself solely with the results, rather than with the mechanisms used to accomplish those results. What we evaluate is not the artifacts or apparatus of learning, but the outcome. The outcome of learning resides with the learners, not the pens, pencils, chalkboards, whiteboards, hardware, software, or other paraphernalia of learning.

Since we are measuring results rather than mechanisms, we can use this framework to evaluate e-learning, just as we evaluate other forms of learning. There are, however, some reasons why we might want to use different techniques and employ some different technologies to the evaluation process. While this section covers electronic means of evaluating electronically delivered learning, keep in mind that conventional means can be used to evaluate e-learning, just as electronic means can be used to evaluate conventional learning.

Perils of Evaluating E-Learning

If you read nothing else in this section, at least scan this list. It catalogs the most common traps that ensnare those new to evaluating e-learning.

Measuring only what is easy to measure. Online systems simplify the collection and analysis of data points, but success at all levels of evaluation may be more than a checkmark or numerical rating. It is often more subtle and nuanced. It may lie in the relationship among several factors. Let computers and networks collect the data, but apply human wisdom to analyze it.

Not evaluating soon enough. E-learning promises right-now learning. It fuels expectations of instant responses. ("Why haven't you answered the email I sent 10 minutes ago?") If feedback from learners identifies a serious problem, fix it immediately.

Evaluating too soon. Effects at Levels 3 and 4 take time to accrue and manifest. Trying to evaluate them immediately after e-learning (or any learning) can confuse and frustrate learners.

Asking invalid test questions. Suppose that a significant number of learners get test question 27 wrong. Is this a failure to learn, or a flawed test question? If the latter, revise the question and restart data gathering.

Not evaluating both the team and the individual. Most learning aims to elevate entire groups of people. Most work is performed by teams. So, craft your evaluation techniques to capture both the results of the team and the contribution of the individual.

Failing to evaluate in the data giver's medium of choice. What is the most convenient and natural way for those performing evaluation (learners and others) to answer your questions? One obvious medium is the one in which learning was offered. Learners should be able to evaluate e-learning via electronic means, typically using tools in the learning management system that delivered the course. Learners and others will be more responsive if they can provide evaluation by media they are most familiar with; for example, paper forms, online surveys, text messaging on smartphones, and even screen taps on smartwatches.

Making evaluation a burden. Don't be a pest to those supplying you with feedback. Remember, to them, evaluation is just more busy work. Don't nag or threaten them if they are slow completing evaluation forms. Trim lists of questions so that completing the form fits in the quantum of the evaluator's patience. And remember, e-learning attracts impatient people in busy organizations.

Comparing e-learning to unevaluated classroom learning. Consider the following dialogue:

> MANAGER: Is our e-learning course as good as the classroom version?
> EVALUATOR: How good is the classroom course?
> MANAGER: It works perfectly.
> EVALUATOR: Oh, you've evaluated it recently?
> MANAGER: No! I told you it works fine.
> EVALUATOR: I'll get back to you. [Exits at a run.]

Releasing the trolls. In evaluation, balance anonymity and accountability. Sometimes, but not often, online discussions go horribly wrong when insecure individuals, cloaked in electronic anonymity, say things they would never say otherwise. Watch out for extreme criticism, emotional language, and outright lies—like in a political debate.

Exhibiting the blank-slate effect. Because e-learning is new to some organizations, they may take a from-scratch approach at evaluation, forgetting or ignoring everything they have learned about learning and evaluation. Nothing about e-learning invalidates anything in the other parts of this book.

Evaluating Level 1: Reaction

Even today, e-learning is a new experience for many learners. For it to succeed, it must overcome natural skepticism and inertia. Level 1 evaluation helps us to monitor emotional acceptance of e-learning, and it can be essential in gathering the testimonials and statistics to generate a positive buzz around e-learning.

So how do you evaluate response electronically? Here are some suggestions.

Let learners vote on course design. Online polls and ballots give learners the opportunity to comment on aspects of e-learning design and delivery. In live virtual-classroom sessions, you can use the built-in polling feature to ask for immediate feedback on the quality of presentation and delivery. Such ballots can record scores over a period of time.

In addition to polling tools that may be part of a conferencing or learning management system, there are some well-known stand-alone tools, such as Survey Monkey (surveymonkey.com), Poll Daddy (polldaddy.com), and Poll Everywhere (polleverywhere.com). Also, Google "online survey or polling tools" to see even more tools.

Set up a course discussion thread. Let learners talk about their experiences taking e-learning. One way to do this is to set up a course discussion forum. Such a forum serves as a bulletin board where designers can post questions or issues to which learners can respond. Discussion forums are a common feature within online meeting tools and are also available as stand-alone online discussion tools.

The following example shows entries on one such forum that asks learners to evaluate one aspect of the course design (Figure 9-1).

In such discussions, learners can see other learners' comments and respond to them, creating an ongoing conversation that reveals more than a simple vote or numeric rating.

Figure 9-1. Course Discussion Forum Example

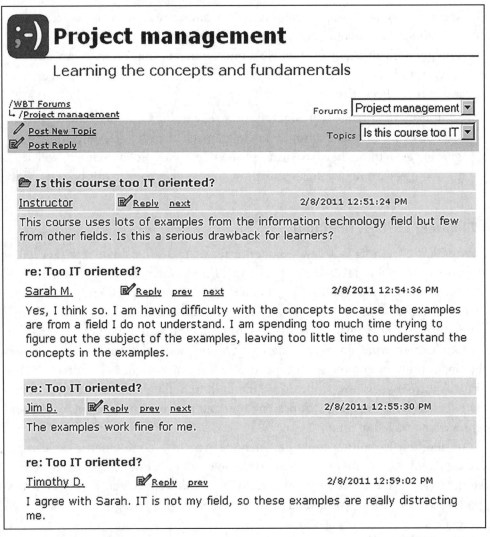

Instead of a discussion forum, you may prefer to use a blog (or wiki) that posts entries as an ongoing journal of comments. Blogs can be more spontaneous; discussion forums, more structured. Try both and see which harvests the kinds of comments you're after.

In either case, be sure to seed the conversation with questions that provoke meaningful discussion. Avoid questions that ask little more than "Did you like it?"

Many learning management systems (LMSs) have some kind of forum component. Some hosted and stand-alone options include UBB Forum, phpBB, and ProBoards.

Use chat or instant messaging for a focus group. Focus groups traditionally required a lot of travel and set-up time. With chat and instant messaging, travel is no longer required. Participants just all join a chat session, and each person in the session sees the comments typed by the others. Brainstorming is especially suited for chat because it encourages a free flow of many ideas without criticism.

You could conduct focus groups with telephone conferencing, but chat has the advantage of leaving behind a written record with no notes to transcribe.

If you have access to an online meeting tool, such as WebEx, Go-To-Meeting, or Google Hangouts, you can conduct a conventional focus group with voice, video, and shared display areas. If you do use such a tool, record the session so you can play it back for further analysis and for taking notes.

Gather feedback frequently. With e-learning, you can embed evaluation events among the learning experiences and ask for respondents to provide reasoning for their feedback. This approach can reveal unanticipated reactions, such as a learner who did not like or dislike the lesson but was surprised at what it contained.

More frequent evaluations also solve the problem of e-learners who drop out before reaching the end of the course and therefore don't make it to the end-of-course evaluation.

When using these types of frequent mini-evaluations, keep them short and simple, with only a question or two. Never subject the learner to a lengthy interrogation as a reward for completing a tough module.

Gather feedback continuously. My personal choice is to enable feedback at any time throughout the learning experience. A button can be included on every screen that lets learners immediately comment on the e-learning or ask a question about it. Here is an example of how one system responds to such a button (Figure 9-2).

Providing the ability to send feedback at any time lets learners report problems, confusion, insights, and triumphs immediately. It prevents frustration from building to the point that the end-of-course or end-of-lesson evaluation becomes an emotional rant. It also provides an early warning of problems so you can fix them. By the time the sixth learner encounters the problem area, it's been fixed.

Record meaningful statistics automatically. Web servers, virtual-classroom systems, LMSs, and learning content management systems (LCMSs) all record detailed

Figure 9-2. Continuous Feedback Example

Send a comment

Who do you want the message to go to?
```
Instructor
```

Your message:
```
Where I work, we are using a very good book
about graphics for electronic documents. I
would like to see it on our list of
resources. It is available from Amazon.com
```

Your name (optional):
```
Lucinda
```

Your e-mail address (if you want a reply):
```
lucinda@ergoglyphics.com
```

Attachment (optional):
```
                                        Browse...
```

```
Send
```

© William Horton

information about what the learner did while taking e-learning. By examining logs and reports from such systems, useful data can be gathered, such as:

- frequency and pattern of accessing the course
- number of pages or modules accessed
- assignments submitted
- participation in online chats and discussions
- rate of progress through the course
- answers to polling questions.

When reviewing such data, look for trends and anomalies. You might notice that learners gradually pick up speed as they proceed through a course. Or you might notice that 50 percent of course dropouts occur immediately after Lesson 6. So either Lesson 6 needs improvement, or maybe six lessons are enough for most learners.

Evaluating Level 2: Learning

E-learning greatly simplifies evaluating Level 2. In e-learning, tests can be automatically administered, scored, recorded, and reported. Automatic testing reduces the difficulty, effort, and costs of creating and administering tests. That means you can use tests more widely, such as:

- **pre-tests** to see if learners are ready to begin a course or module
- **diagnostic tests** to identify the specific modules or learning objects learners should take
- **post-tests** to confirm learning or shift learners to remedial learning experiences
- **tests within course modules** to help learners continually monitor accomplishment of learning objectives.

E-learning provides course authors with inexpensive and easy-to-use tools to create tests and standards-based reporting mechanisms to record and report scores (Table 9-1). Some advanced e-learning applications also use testing results to design custom learning programs. Most LMSs and LCMSs also include tools for creating and delivering tests.

Table 9-1. Traditional Testing Tools

Well-known authoring tools that include a testing component	Well-known hosted tools for creating and delivering tests
iSpring Quiz Maker (ispringsolutions.com)	Questionmark Perception (questionmark.com)
Articulate Storyline (articulate.com)	ClassMarker (classmarker.com)
Adobe Captivate (adobe.com)	QuizStar (quizstar.4teachers.org)
Lector Publisher or Inspire (Trivantis.com)	
SumTotal Toolbook (tb.sumtotalsystems.com)	
Elucidat (elucidat.com)—cloud-based	

Level 2.5 Evaluations?

No, there is no Level 2.5, but we can make evaluation of learning more predictive of application. The technique is simple. Rather than testing the recall of knowledge, instead measure the ability to apply knowledge in realistic situations.

Here is an example from a course on food safety. Learners must make a decision about what to do with the exposed cooked turkey. To make that decision, they must gather information from the scene by clicking on objects to enlarge them, or by clicking on people to question them. For example, clicking on the chef reveals the

Figure 9-3. Food Safety Simulation Example

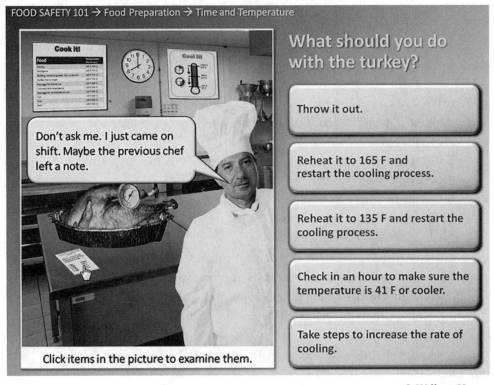

© *William Horton*

response shown and prompts the learner to examine the note mentioned by the chef (Figure 9-3). The learner must gather the same information in the simulation as in the real-world situation.

What kind of tools can be used to build these scenario-based quizzes? Most of the well-known authoring tools listed previously that can create tests allow users to create scenario-based quizzes and branching simulations, most notably Articulate Storyline and Adobe Captivate.

Don't forget about games. Using a game-like format, such as a familiar television quiz show, can make tests less intimidating and more engaging, and perhaps elicit better performance from the learner. The advent of serious games and simulations also presents an opportunity to create realistic situations to increase learning and skills practice.

Standards-Based Score Reporting

E-learning standards for communications between learning content and management systems promise that content developed in different authoring tools can deliver tests and report scores back to any management system, provided all the tools and content follow the same standard. There are three main standards in use today: AICC, SCORM, and Experience API.

The oldest among these main standards is the Aviation Industry Computer-Based Training Committee (AICC). Though originally formed to serve airframe manufacturers, suppliers, and buyers, the AICC has expanded its base to include many other organizations producing and using e-learning content. It is a rich and complex standard that allows designers to designate complex flows through content. However, many developers complain that this standard is hard to implement and that it does not encourage reuse of already-defined lower-level modules. The organization disbanded in 2014; however, the standards are still supported by many LMS vendors and course-authoring tools.

The next member of this elite standards club is the Advanced Distributed Learning (ADL) group's Sharable Content Object Reference Model (SCORM) project. It was established in 1997. SCORM claims that it does not author standards but will adopt and make practical the best standards put forth by the other groups. However, SCORM originally defined its own packaging standard, then in Version 1.2 adopted the IMS Content and Packaging Standard virtually intact. (IMS Global Learning Consortium is yet another standards body.) The SCORM standard addresses issues such as interoperability, portability, reusability, and sequencing. Its current version is SCORM 2004 4th Edition (www.adlnet.gov).

Experience API, also known as xAPI, or more commonly known as Tin Can API, is under the aegis of ADL. It is a technology designed to capture learning data from many types of learning experiences across multiple devices in a consistent format.

The advantage these e-learning standards create for evaluation is that the tedious and expensive process of distributing, conducting, gathering, grading, and recording tests is automated from start to finish. The effort and costs of tests are reduced, and the results of testing are available for immediate analysis.

The exact procedure varies considerably from tool to tool, but once the content is set up, each time a learner answers a test question, that score is recorded in the management system.

Manage Competence

Many large organizations are going beyond simply recording test scores. They are using the immediate availability of test results to continuously guide learning in their organizations to ensure that targeted competencies are achieved.

Some LMSs and knowledge management tools are connecting testing and e-learning to more precisely target competencies needed by learners. The learner might be faced with a large, extensive course that takes many hours to complete. Desiring a more efficient learning experience that takes into account what he or she already knows, the learner clicks on the Customize button.

The learner engages in a test to identify gaps in knowledge and skills. The result of the test is a custom course consisting of just the modules the learner needs. The learner can now begin a custom learning program that targets his or her competency gap with fewer but more specific modules.

Evaluating Level 3: Behavior and Level 4: Results

Since application and results occur outside of the e-learning course itself, their evaluation is less coupled to the e-learning or to the technologies needed for it. That means that the same mechanisms used for any other type of learning can be used to evaluate Levels 3 and 4.

How to Evaluate Informal Learning

By Saul Carliner

Informal learning "refers to situations in which some combination of the process, location, purpose, and content of instruction are determined by the worker, who may or may not be conscious that an instructional event occurred" (Carliner 2012).

Examples of informal learning include reading books and watching online videos about a subject to master it; participating in a structured on-the-job training program; working with a mentor, either through a formal program or on a casual basis; and picking up lessons through informal conversations with co-workers at lunch and during breaks.

This section explores ways to evaluate informal learning. It first identifies unique challenges of evaluating informal learning, and then suggests ways to adapt the four levels to respond to these challenges.

Challenges of Evaluating Informal Learning

As with formal learning, training and development professionals often seek to quantify the amount of learning that occurs informally, as well as its impact. Unfortunately, approaches used to evaluate formal learning are ineffective with informal learning.

Informal Learning Occurs Outside of Formally Scheduled Events

First, the definition of informal learning suggests that it usually occurs outside of formally scheduled events. When informal learning does occur during a formally scheduled event, it is usually an event that has a purpose other than learning, such as a department meeting or trade show. These events, especially meetings, often do not lend themselves easily to evaluation, making Level 1 Reaction evaluation difficult, if not impossible.

Informal Learning Lacks Formal Learning Objectives

Second, informal learning lacks formal learning objectives. Even when learners engage in self-directed informal learning activities, they rarely have formal learning objectives. Learners establish their own goals, which rarely resemble the observable, measurable objectives prepared for formal learning programs that are essential to writing effective tests and assessing transfer.

Learners Determine When They Have Finished Learning

The third practical issue affecting the evaluation of informal learning is that learners determine for themselves when they have finished learning, which often occurs before they have actually acquired new skills and knowledge. Learners stop learning when they feel they know something, whether or not they have finished the learning activity or have formally verified that they have mastered the new skills and knowledge. This further complicates efforts to assess Level 2 Learning and Level 3 Behavior. It also complicates efforts to assess Level 4 Results because learning is an individual rather than a collective activity.

Net Investment Cannot Be Tracked

The fourth practical issue is that much informal learning uses existing resources, requiring no net investment that can be tracked.

Informal Learning Is Unconscious

The last practical issue is that although traditional evaluation efforts suppose that learning occurs consciously, much informal learning is unconscious (Wihak et al. 2008 and Marsick and Watkins 2011). If people do not realize that they learned anything, no trigger occurs to begin the evaluation process.

Adapting the Kirkpatrick Model to Address the Challenges of Informal Learning

As a result of these issues, the Kirkpatrick Model must be adapted to evaluate informal learning. Specifically, consider these adjustments to the Kirkpatrick framework.

Evaluating Informal Learning at Level 1

Informal learning occurs unconsciously through self-directed activities and events intended for purposes other than learning. Therefore, evaluators need to find out which resources learners use for learning, and the extent to which they use them, so they know to what stimulus the reaction actually refers. Furthermore, because learners might consult several resources to learn a single subject, merely assessing use of and satisfaction with individual resources provides an incomplete picture, so evaluations need to take a more holistic approach. Here are some specific suggestions:

- Track use of various resources that might be employed for informal learning. For information-based resources, such as online documentation, micro-sites, and mobile applications, use web analytics to track use. For event-based resources, track attendance or participation.
- On published resources, include a two-question satisfaction survey, such as Microsoft does on its help pages. One question asks whether or not the online material addressed the learners' needs (for simplicity and clarity, use yes/no rather than a broader scale), and the other asks learners to explain their response, which is especially useful if the resource fails to meet the learners' needs. The feedback provides insights into how to better align the material with users' needs.
- For events, distribute a typical satisfaction survey, but explicitly ask participants whether or not they learned anything (make this, too, a yes/no question), and, if so, ask what they learned.
- To assess broader participation in and satisfaction with informal learning, include questions about these issues on employee surveys (and, for training groups that provide customer training, customer surveys). To get a sense of which resources people use, provide a list of 5 to 10 resources and ask participants how often they use them (such as never, once a week, once a month, once a quarter). To get a sense of reaction, ask learners whether they feel they have the resources needed to learn for their jobs, whether they feel comfortable learning during work hours (some research, such as Lim and Morris 2006 and Skule 2004, suggests that workers do not feel this way), and whether they feel that informal learning is appropriate or is only being used because no formal training is available.

Evaluating Informal Learning at Level 2

Because informal learners set their own objectives, express them vaguely, and determine for themselves when they have finished learning, formal tests of objectives from an instructor are not possible. However, you should provide self-assessments and encourage learners to take them for these reasons: informal learners ultimately hope to develop skills their employers will recognize; research suggests that learners are poor assessors of their own skill level (Sitzmann, Brown, and Bauer 2010); and for your own assessment of the effectiveness of various learning resources.

Self-assessments are written like tests of formal learning. To determine what to assess, identify specific skills that informal learners might try to develop in a particular subject area and use them as the basis of assessment. Because learners might be reticent to take a self-assessment unless assured of anonymity, only track scores. Do not record scores for individual learners or report scores of individual learners to management (in fact, sever the link between a learner and a self-assessment score).

Evaluating Informal Learning at Level 3

Because the aggregated effect of informal learning occurs through the variety of experiences in which learners participated and resources to which they were exposed, Level 3 is probably the most significant of all of the levels of evaluation. It shows not only transfer to the job, but also how learners synthesized learning from so many resources.

The most direct means of assessing Level 3 is certification (Carliner 2012), which is defined as the validation of competence in a particular family of skills by an independent third party (Hale 2011). The ideal form of certification is an annotated portfolio, which lets learners not only show their work, but also describe it. The description provides insights into the ways in which workers have adopted what they learned in their everyday work.

The performance evaluation process provides another means of assessing learning transfer. When writing the evaluation, managers can consider how workers have evolved in their jobs since the last appraisal, such as whether they have adopted new techniques and technologies, can handle a broader range of assignments, or have changed their approaches. The ensuing conversation provides managers with an opportunity to identify what workers have learned and how they have integrated it into their work. Compiling notes from evaluations of several workers in a particular department or function provides insights into broader informal learning processes in those groups.

Evaluating Informal Learning at Level 4

As with any type of learning, attempts to assess the impact of specific informal learning, especially the financial returns, are ultimately futile. Rather, organizations can assess the overall impact of informal learning by exploring broad metrics of departmental, functional, or organizational effectiveness. If the organization tracks metrics associated with innovation, track those, too. If they have changed, one issue to consider is the impact of informal learning on those changes.

Although stakeholders would hope that the metrics demonstrate improvement, in some instances, they might suggest otherwise. For example, some evidence suggests that organizations in general have gently reduced their investments in training over the past several decades when adjusted for inflation (Carliner and Bakir 2010), and have increased their reliance on informal learning (Hughes and Campbell 2009; Hughes and Grant 2007). Evaluating these metrics can assess the success of such a strategy.

References

Carliner, S. 2012. *Informal Learning Basics*. Alexandria, VA: ASTD Press.

Carliner, S., and I. Bakir. 2010. "Trends in Spending on Training: An Analysis of the 1982 Through 2008 Training Annual Industry Reports." *Performance Improvement Quarterly*, 23:3, 77–105.

Grant, M., and P.D. Hughes. 2007. "Learning and Development Outlook 2007: Are We Learning Enough?" The Conference Board of Canada, April 23.

Hale, J. 2011. *Performance-Based Certification: How to Design a Valid, Defensible, Cost-Effective Program.* 2nd ed. San Francisco, CA: Pfeiffer.

Howard, A., and P.D. Hughes, 2009. "Learning and Development Outlook 2009: Learning in Tough Times." The Conference Board of Canada, August 11.

Lim, D. H., and M.L. Morris. 2006. "Influence of Trainee Characteristics, Instructional Satisfaction, and Organizational Climate on Perceived Learning and Training Transfer." *Human Resource Development Quarterly*, 17:1, 85–115.

Marsick, V. J., and K. Watkins. 2011. "Pursuing Research in Organizations That Is Useful to Practice." Academy of Human Resource Development International Research Conference in the Americas. Schaumburg, IL, February 24.

Sitzmann, T., K. Ely, K.G. Brown, and K.N. Bauer. 2010. "Self-Assessment of Knowledge: A Cognitive Learning or Affective Measure?" *Academy of Management Learning & Education*, 9:2, 169–191.

Skule, S. 2004. "Learning Conditions at Work: A Framework to Understand and Assess Informal Learning in the Workplace." *International Journal of Training and Development*, 8:1, 8–20.

Wihak, C., G. Hall, J. Bratton, L. Warkentin, L. Wihak, and S. MacPherson. 2008. Unpublished report. *Work-Related Informal Learning: Research and Practice in the Canadian Context.* Ottawa, ON: Work and Learning Knowledge Centre of the Canadian Centre for Learning.

How to Evaluate Mobile Learning

By Clark Quinn

The New World Kirkpatrick Model, while promoted for evaluating training, is by no means limited to that application. The principle behind starting with the end goal and working backwards, looking at the needed change and the effectiveness of an intervention to instigate that change, holds for any sort of organizational intervention involving people. For example, you could apply the model to evaluate compensation packages, new work processes, and even mobile learning (m-learning).

Defining Mobile Learning

M-learning is about using mobile devices to make ourselves more effective wherever we are, and at any time. Mobile devices can be defined from wearables to tablets (laptops don't qualify because they can't naturally be used while standing or walking). The prototypical device, however, the one you have with you all the time, is the smartphone or pocketable. This forms a basis for considering m-learning.

M-learning provides a good test case for use of the Kirkpatrick Model to evaluate something other than traditional learning because it covers a multitude of solutions. By consensus, the expert opinion is that m-learning is not about courses on a phone. Instead, the usage pattern of mobile devices (many quick, short accesses versus fewer, longer accesses on a laptop) supports different ways of assisting learners. It is very much about "just-in-time" assistance versus a "just-in-case" approach. At a higher level, two major categories arise in this view of m-learning: 1) augmenting formal learning; and 2) supporting performance (Quinn 2011). Each of these has facets that need to be understood if m-learning is to be evaluated appropriately.

Even if courses are not being delivered, the learning experience can be extended in several ways. For one, we know that learning works better if it is spaced over time. Therefore, mobile can serve as a channel to provide a continuing stream of concept presentations, examples, and practice opportunities, extending the learning experience. From the Kirkpatrick perspective, this is not unique; it's a component of the New World Level 3. In m-learning, then, Levels 3 and 4 proceed as normal, but we also have the opportunity to consider using mobile in particular ways at each level.

Evaluating Level 1 for M-Learning

Mobile devices can be used to administer Level 1 assessments at any time. Conferences are already using mobile devices to present information and notifications and are now beginning to use surveys to collect attendee feedback. Beyond participating in the learning experience, learners can be polled on their experience.

Evaluating Level 2 for M-Learning

Mobile devices can also be used for Level 2. Similar to and in addition to the methods used for e-learning, simulations can be delivered on mobile devices and through alternate-reality scenarios (simulations distributed in the real world). Contextual performance can be addressed as well, using relevant information triggered by a learner's proximity to a location or an event.

For instance, if we are near a location specific to the organization's and learner's goals, we can bring up appropriate information to reactivate learning, or even ask the learner to make the connection. We can also run a task that helps learners familiarize themselves with a locale, such as a physical plant, on a mobile scavenger hunt.

Similarly, if a learner engages in an activity that is part of a learning goal, material can be provided to reactivate knowledge, or reflection support could be triggered to connect the learner to an evaluation resource or a mentor. In cases in which information is simply presented, that, too, can be tracked as part of the larger learning exposure. In cases in which learners actually take an evaluation or perform, those steps can be part of the overall assessment.

Evaluating Level 3 for M-Learning

Just as with Level 2, at Level 3 it is easier to check if the desired behavior is occurring, particularly in situations in which performance happens outside of the workplace. Just as performance after learning can be evaluated, so too can ongoing performance be determined. Any individual observing the learner can be polled or respond on mobile devices. This decouples Level 3 from the workplace and makes it more flexible. Also, we can augment the performance environment to actually record whether behaviors are happening. Additionally, the mobile device itself can report if, when, and how it is being used.

Whether the solution is developed as an app, accessed via mobile web, or some solution in between, what is often impractical is to actually observe Level 3 in action, because the whole point is that it happens when the individual is in motion. While we can shadow a sample of the population and see if they are using the solution, which isn't a bad form of triangulation, we have another resource as well. We can technologically track any use of the device in several ways.

Any mobile web solution can, of course, be tracked by any traditional website tracking, such as Google Analytics. Or, if the solution is accessing data, the data server can provide usage information. More important, within a mobile app, the software can be instrumented to report on usage. While this traditionally has required creating one's own reporting format, the Advanced Distributed Learning initiative of the U.S. Department of Defense has created a standard that allows reporting of actions in a consistent way, the Experience API (Application Programming Interface), or xAPI for short. This is a simple syntax that can be put into the mobile app and aggregated through a Learning Record Store (LRS). If not yet, there soon will be development tools that provide this as a core capability.

Performance support is a related case, and yet a more natural match to mobile. Here, we are not concerned with whether the individual learns anything; instead, whether the task gets accomplished. For example, if a person needs to know a particular product feature, that person can look it up, and that access can be tracked. In fact, in situations in which the product features are volatile, changing frequently, it would make more sense to not learn any particular configuration.

Another situation is accessing a video or document on troubleshooting and repair. An individual might use the support resource to solve an issue the first time it occurs but still need to access the resource for the same issue when it occurs again. That's okay. For example, the checklists created for medical procedures are to be accessed even if users trust their own medical education because the checklists compensate for a very human circumstance to occasionally forget or skip a step. So, how do we evaluate mobile performance support?

Evaluating Level 4 for M-Learning

Evaluation of Level 4 does not change for m-learning or performance support. As with all interventions, evaluators should have an idea of what metric needs to be shifted. Work backwards to Level 3, where you determine what support would likely lead to behavior that will move that needle. Then work back to Level 2 and make sure that the individuals know both how to use the mobile solution and the contexts in which it is to be used, and that they are confident and committed. Finally, you can determine whether the individuals are satisfied with the solution's usability and availability.

Putting It All Together

The overall process looks like this (Figure 9-4):

- **Level 4:** A mobile solution is developed that can positively affect a needed business metric.
- **Level 3:** Usage is tracked and/or stakeholders surveyed to see whether the mobile solution is being used.
- **Level 2:** Individuals demonstrate the ability to successfully use the solution and understand the use cases, and their commitment and confidence can be surveyed.
- **Level 1:** The users are surveyed about their experience with the mobile solution; for example, its usability and availability.

In practice, work from Level 4 down to Level 3, determining a solution to the need and an implementation plan. From there, evaluate Levels 1 and 2 in traditional or digital ways. Then, work back up to Level 3 to determine if you are seeing the necessary behavior, through observation or device data, before seeing at Level 4 if the desired impact has been achieved. Naturally, evaluation should be used iteratively and formatively to determine and fine-tune success before being used summatively to document the outcome.

Evaluating Social Access

Interestingly, another role of m-learning is social access. Most mobile devices support a suite of communication channels, including voice, text message (SMS/MMS), and social apps. Most corporate social tools have a mobile solution as well. This suggests

Figure 9-4. Putting It All Together

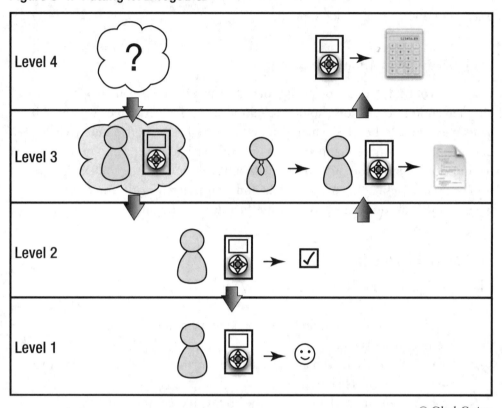

© *Clark Quinn*

that there may be a reason to use the four levels to evaluate social and informal learning.

Much of the evaluation of social learning discusses intangibles: if there is activity and the right culture and facilitation, good things will come without having to be specific (Bingham and Conner 2015). Here, the only metric is whether or not people are using the system, a Level 3 outcome, and there is faith that this leads to good outcomes at Level 4. However, also consider cases where social is used in specific ways, anticipate the impact and use the model to both improve and demonstrate the outcome. Problem solving, design, and research are all situations in which the answer is not known at the outset; consequently, these are learning situations, too. In times of change, these types of situations are of increasing importance to the success of the organization. So you could and should consider how you might systematically evaluate these circumstances.

On a business unit by business unit basis, the benefits of increased interaction can be anticipated. In sales, for instance, time to close might be decreased and closure rates might be increased. In operations, errors might be reduced; processes or other concrete outcomes might be improved. The point is that there are likely tangible outcomes, and if there are tangible anticipated outcomes, the Kirkpatrick Model can be applied with some modifications.

For instance, social could be introduced in the L&D department itself. As a result, the time to produce a course would be expected to be reduced, or the quality of course outcomes or the success rate would increase. Level 2 assesses whether learners know how to use the system and social skills. Level 3 gauges activity, and Level 4 employs unit metrics. Other factors exist outside of the intervention, such as whether the culture makes it safe to share and there's a commitment to "show your work" (Bozarth 2014); however, if you demonstrate the ability to use the system at Level 2 and there isn't activity at Level 3, the problem is likely the culture or other barriers.

References

Bingham, T., and M. Conner. 2015. *The New Social Learning: Connect. Collaborate. Work.* 2nd ed. Alexandria, VA: ATD Press.

Bozarth, J. 2014. *Show Your Work: The Payoffs and How-To's of Working Out Loud.* San Francisco, CA: Pfeiffer.

Quinn, C.N. 2011. *Designing mLearning: Tapping Into the Mobile Revolution for Organizational Performance.* San Francisco, CA: Pfeiffer.

———. 2014. *Revolutionize Learning & Development: Performance and Innovation Strategy for the Information Age.* San Francisco, CA: Wiley.

Summary

The Kirkpatrick Model, interpreted beyond training, provides a valid framework for evaluating all types of interventions, including e-learning, informal learning, mobile learning, and social learning. This is important, as L&D can and should be looking to go "beyond the course" and take responsibility for more elements of success in the organization, including performance support and social or informal learning (Quinn 2014).

Equipped with a viable evaluation framework, interventions of a broader perspective can be developed, improved, and evaluated on a formal basis. Learning professionals can think of different and evolving learning modalities as companions to more traditional learning or as stand-alone modes. The important thing to remember is that all interventions warrant evaluation to ensure that value is being created and demonstrated, and the Kirkpatrick Model is easily adapted as the framework to conduct the evaluation. Equally important, new modes can be used to evaluate traditional learning, and vice versa. Use a broad view when considering what is "learning" and how it will be evaluated so that you make the best use of the resources available to you.

CHAPTER 10

Evaluation Instrument Creation Basics

Matthew Champagne

This chapter provides practical answers to some of the most common questions about how a nonstatistician can create evaluation tools that work and provide credible data. While it is by no means exhaustive, this chapter provides basic guidance that any learning professional can implement; its purpose is to offer solutions to some of the typical structural problems found on evaluation forms that generate ambiguous or misleading results and suppress response rate.

Typical Questions

For more than two decades, trainers and evaluators from every type of learning organization have asked me many of the same questions about surveys, reaction sheets, and evaluation forms:

- Are we asking the right questions? In the right way?
- Is our survey too long?
- Why are our results ambiguous or not interpretable?
- Is there a "best" number of points on our rating scales?
- How do we get higher response rates?

The simple answer is that these questions and many others are addressed by properly applying psychological measurement principles to our surveys. Applying these principles correctly focuses the content, maximizes response rates, engages respondents, and generates meaningful, interpretable results. Ignoring these principles creates ambiguity and artifacts that are not realized until the analysis is conducted.

In other words, those who properly apply psychological measurement principles rarely ask me any of these questions because they don't have these problems. When someone asks one of these questions, it is certain that one or more of the principles was not addressed, and that is the source of the problem. Applying the following steps will prevent misleading results that cost time and money to address.

The Key to Success

If there were unlimited time and resources, each student in the class could be interviewed and asked specific questions to dig deep and learn all that we wished to know. But there are not unlimited resources, so this approach cannot be used. Instead, a survey or evaluation form can be created to serve as a proxy for this detailed interview. Therefore, items and instructions must be created that are clear, unambiguous, and compelling so that the respondents' written responses are captured and interpreted exactly as intended.

This almost never happens.

For most surveys, there is a large gap between the respondents' perceptions and our interpretation of those perceptions based on the responses. Applying the advice in this chapter, however, will significantly narrow that gap and make us confident that the respondents' thoughts and perceptions have been captured and interpreted correctly.

The key to success is to ensure that the content and structure of your items and response scales are consistent with psychological measurement principles. Here are six steps to ensure success.

1. Consider the subjectivity of your response scales.
2. Match the "natures" of items and response scales.
3. Check for unnecessary use of the opt-out option.
4. Don't lump specific numbers into general categories.
5. Choose meaningful categories for your items.
6. Complete the three-point final review.

Step 1: Consider the Subjectivity of Your Response Scales

Here is a response scale that incorrectly assumes all respondents will uniformly interpret the mental distances between the five anchors to be identical (Figure 10-1):

Figure 10-1. Response Scale 1

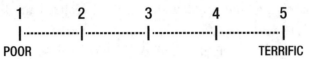

There are two defined anchors (POOR and TERRIFIC) but three undefined anchors. Respondents attach different meanings to undefined anchors, so multiple interpretations of the same scale may exist. Some respondents may interpret the mental distance between anchors to look like this (Figure 10-2):

Figure 10-2. Response Scale 2

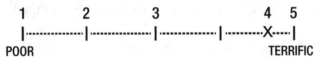

That is, a respondent may see little difference between ratings of 1, 2, or 3 (all are poor) and may choose 3 to indicate that he is not happy. However, the instructor may assume that the respondent chose a 3 to indicate a midscale opinion of "neither good nor bad," so the instructor may not act on the learner's concerns.

Another person may look at the same scale but internally judge the mental distance to look like this (Figure 10-3):

Figure 10-3. Response Scale 3

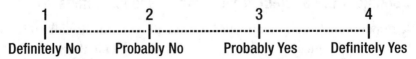

That is, this respondent rarely uses the end points, reserving a 5 only for exceptional cases. Instead, the respondent chooses a 4 to express that she was very pleased, but the instructor wonders why the student was so disappointed and did not choose a 5.

When anchors are not labeled, the responses cannot be accurately summarized because instructors do not know what a 3 or a 4 means to each respondent. Instructors can increase the accuracy of results by labeling anchors with descriptors that are likely to have the same meaning to all respondents. Each descriptor should be clear and unique (Figure 10-4).

Figure 10-4. Response Scale 4

Someone choosing a 3 is expressing an opinion categorically different than someone choosing a 2 or a 4. Each anchor has only one reasonable meaning that is likely to be shared by all respondents; thus, the average results across all respondents are interpretable. Another good example is a five-point Likert-type scale when used correctly with descriptive anchors ranging from Strongly Agree to Strongly Disagree.

Uniquely labeling each anchor becomes increasingly difficult as the number of anchors increases. In such cases, the results will be more interpretable if respondents are guided with meaningful ranges associated with the anchors, as in this example (Figure 10-5):

Figure 10-5. Response Scale 5

How likely is it that you would recommend this course to a colleague?

Not at All Likely	◄-------Unlikely	------Neutral------	Likely----------►	Extremely Likely

| 0 | 1 | 2 | 3 | 4 | 5 | 6 | 7 | 8 | 9 | 10 |

Step 2: Match the "Natures" of Items and Response Scales

Evaluation forms often use the same response scale type for all items, even though it may not "match" all the items. Respondents are left to interpret how the item fits the scale, and the results are often unclear as to what was intended. The most common error is using a five-point Likert-type scale, which represents agreement, but framing the items in terms of quality, frequency, or amount. Here are examples of mismatches (Figure 10-6):

Figure 10-6. Mismatched Items

	Strongly Agree	Agree	Neutral	Disagree	Strongly Disagree
1. I attended sessions regularly.	O	O	O	O	O
2. The pace of the course was satisfactory.	O	O	O	O	O
3. I took advantage of my instructor's office hours.	O	O	O	O	O
4. This course was excellent.	O	O	O	O	O

Item #1 addresses frequency. The survey maker probably wants to know how often respondents attended the sessions, but instead uses the word *regularly* and asks respondents to rate their level of agreement. This leaves the results open to interpretation: if the respondents select "Disagree," how many sessions did they attend? None? All but one? The meaning of "regularly" differs from person to person.

The results of item #2 cannot be interpreted. If a respondent disagrees, the instructor cannot know whether the person's opinion was that the pace of the course was too fast or too slow, and therefore cannot address that concern.

Item #3 is a frequency or a Yes/No item. The survey maker has to decide what is important here—knowing whether a respondent attended office hours at all, or how often. If a respondent selects "Agree," does that mean one time or every week? Respondents who select "Disagree" may have attended as often as others but perceived they had not taken advantage of every opportunity.

Item #4 violates the neutral statement requirement. Using the qualifier "excellent" makes the results difficult to interpret. Some respondents may choose "Agree" as the highest possible rating, meaning that they agree that the experience was indeed excellent. Those interpreting the results will think they were not fully satisfied, however, because Agree is a 4 on a 5-point scale. This is an artifact of a mismatch between item and response scale. Do not use qualifiers (for example, great or outstanding) that will be redundant with the response scale.

Each item on your survey must be considered in terms of the response scale that fits the item. Is the question about quality? If so, then a scale ranging from "Excellent" to "Poor" is appropriate. Is the question about frequency? If so, then a scale ranging from "Always" to "Never" may be best. Is the question about preference? Speed or strength? Level of difficulty? Amount? Each of these types of questions requires a different response scale. Matching the natures of items and response scales ensures that the questions are asked the right way. Here are four common question types with appropriate matching response scales (Figure 10-7):

Figure 10-7. Four Common Question Types

Agreement	Likelihood	Frequency	Quality
Strongly Agree	Definitely Yes	Always	Excellent
Agree	Probably Yes	Often	Very Good
Neither Agree nor Disagree	Probably No	Sometimes	Good
Disagree	Definitely No	Never	Fair
Strongly Disagree			Poor

Step 3: Check for Unnecessary Use of the Opt-Out Option

Reaction sheets often contain an option labeled "Not Applicable." This choice is appropriate when respondents may not have the information or experience to answer; however, the opt-out choice should be used strategically and not provided as an option for all items. Allowing respondents to skip questions for which they certainly hold an opinion results in loss of valuable information.

Here are two examples (Figure 10-8):

Figure 10-8. Two Example Questions with Unnecessary Opt-Outs

	Excellent	Good	Fair	Poor	Not Applicable
1. Overall, my experience in this course was:	O	O	O	O	O

	Strongly Agree	Agree	Disagree	Strongly Disagree	Not Applicable
2. I enjoyed this instructor's communication style:	O	O	O	O	O

In both of these cases, the respondent has certainly had an experience and can provide some feedback. For item #1, the individual did attend the class. The student may not have participated much and may not have attended every session, but must have some opinion, which is what you are soliciting. Providing a Not Applicable option allows the respondent to prevent you from learning that opinion.

In item #2, all students in the training session listened to the instructor and must have formed some opinion of whether or not they liked the instructor's communication style. Providing a Not Applicable option forfeits valuable information, and it is not clear what was intended with their response.

The Not Applicable option is fine for questions about measures of performance that may not have been administered or course materials that may not have been distributed, but all students should provide an opinion on characteristics of the instructor and course. In all cases, judicious use of the Not Applicable option will provide more useful data and more interpretable results.

Step 4: Don't Lump Specific Numbers Into General Categories

One way to lose information on a survey is by turning ordinal or interval data into nominal data—lumping specific numbers into poorly defined categories.

Consider this question: "How many online training courses have you attended this year?"

Although there may be a specific and meaningful answer (for example, "I've attended seven courses"), this is not learned because only these choices are offered (Figure 10-9):

Figure 10-9. Arbitrary Groups Example

How many online training courses have you attended this year?

○ 0

○ 1–4

○ 5–8

○ More than 8

Rather than learn the true answer ("7 courses"), the survey maker only knows that the answer falls between 5 and 8. In the analysis, when numbers are grouped, all values within that group are treated as equal.

This is not done in daily conversations. If asked, "How many scoops of ice cream do you want?" you would not reply, "Between one and four please." You might say, "Two scoops." If asked, "How tall are you?" you would not reply, "Between 5'4" and 5'10". You might say, "I am 5 foot, 7 inches."

Ask questions in just the same way on your reaction sheets to learn the specific answer:

How many online training courses have you attended this year? _____

By not forcing respondents to translate their actual answer into an arbitrary category, you may also discover interesting findings in data that were previously hidden due to this structural artifact. To learn what respondents are truly thinking, prompt for specific answers that will give you specific and useful results.

Step 5: Choose Meaningful Categories for Your Items

In situations in which you must use categories and are unable to ask open-ended questions that would yield specific answers, be sure to use categories that have meaning based on introspection or historical data. In the analysis, all choices within the group are treated as equal, so the categories should be defined so that there is more similarity within groups than between groups (Figure 10-10).

With this phrasing, respondents with zero experience are seen as "equal" in the analysis to respondents with three years of experience (both experience levels are coded as a 1 in the analysis). Those with 11 years of experience are treated the same as those with 30 years of experience. If that is not reasonable, then reconsider these groupings.

For example, looking through historical data, such as past administrations of the same survey or membership records, you may find that the range of experience for

Figure 10-10. Example of Arbitrary Groupings

How many years of experience do you have?

O 0–3 years
O 4–6 years
O 7–10 years
O More than 10 years

everyone in your sample extends from 1 year to 29 years. Further, you may discover that only a handful of people have more than 20 years of experience. Armed with this information, you might add a category and revise (Figure 10-11):

Figure 10-11. Better Example of Groupings

How many years of experience do you have?

O 1–5 years
O 6–10 years
O 11–15 years
O 16–20 years
O More than 20 years

Thinking further, you may realize that most of your participants must take a certification exam after four years; therefore, there is something categorically different about those with five years of experience versus those with four years. You also may discover in previous data collected that few individuals have 14 to 20 years of experience, and disproportionately more have five to eight years of experience. Perhaps there is something different about those individuals who remain members beyond their eighth year or those with 14 or more years. You revise accordingly (Figure 10-12):

Figure 10-12. Best Example of Groupings

How many years of experience do you have?

O 1–4 years
O 5–8 years
O 9–13 years
O 14–20 years
O More than 20 years

All figures © Matthew Champagne

Inspecting charts or tables displaying the results with these more meaningful groupings provides the opportunity to take the proper corrective action. If categories must be used, review previous surveys or historical data to thoughtfully consider the ranges of values possible for each group until the categories are meaningful.

Step 6: Complete the Three-Point Final Review

Before distributing a survey, take these three actions to identify gaps and problem areas:

Action #1: Pretend you are the busy and important person who will be taking your survey. Carefully read every word, especially the instructions. Are you convinced it is worthwhile? Is anything confusing or ambiguous? Are there any incidents of improper jargon? Would you want to fill out your own survey? Most problems with low engagement can be eliminated by looking at the survey content from the perspective of the respondents.

Action #2: Think of how the items could be interpreted and how the results will be analyzed (that is, begin with the end in mind). What if 90 percent of respondents choose the same answer for a question? What if there are two choices that no one selects? If respondents choose "N/A" or "Agree" or "Fair," is it clear what they are trying to express, or could that response have multiple meanings? Is there so much complexity in the survey that the analysis will be too difficult to perform? Taking time to imagine different scenarios in the results will force you to consider the survey content so that the analysis is efficient and meaningful.

Action #3: Pilot test. Whenever possible, cross-check your work from Action #1 and Action #2 by administering your survey to a small, representative sample of participants or to a group of your colleagues. Have them explain any unexpected responses given and point out any areas on the survey that needed multiple readings to understand. This will help identify misunderstandings and remove obstacles before you launch.

Summary

You do not have to be a statistician to create valid survey and interview questions. By applying these six steps to each survey, reaction sheet, and evaluation form, you will be confident that you are maximizing your response rate and asking the right questions in the right way, and that you have a survey of ideal length and structure that yields clear and interpretable results.

CHAPTER 11

Blended Evaluation® Items and Sample Tools

We hope you have not skipped right to this chapter to get "the form," because a standardized evaluation form that works in all circumstances does not exist. Rather, evaluation forms and tools are built based on program needs, combined with the key principles outlined in this book.

The Blended Evaluation® Approach

Many training professionals have evaluated multiple levels within the same tool and do not even realize it, or perhaps believe it is an error. On the contrary, an approach in which multiple levels are evaluated from numerous perspectives is an excellent way to maximize data while minimizing resources on the part of both the training department and the people being queried.

Generally speaking, all evaluation tools should be blended, except in unusual circumstances. This prevents "surveying people out" because you can obtain quite a bit of data with one tool and are not solely reliant on one type of evaluation method.

Instead of "doing a Level 1" after a training program, create a Blended Evaluation® Form in which you ask questions related to all dimensions of Level 1, questions about confidence and commitment to apply what was learned on the job (from Level 2), and questions related to anticipated application and outcomes. This not only makes good use of training evaluation resources but also reduces the focus on the less important Level 1 and proactively provides clues as to what is in store when training graduates return to the job and attempt to apply what they learned.

Similarly, when designing tools for delayed evaluation after training, consider what information will be useful to the training department and important to stakeholders at all four levels. In a delayed evaluation, you primarily want to focus on how training graduates have applied what they learned, what support they are receiving on the job (Level 3), and what kinds of results they have accomplished (Level 4). Sometimes it will be appropriate to ask participants to think back to the training after having had the opportunity to apply what they learned, and to have them reassess the value of the program (Level 1).

This table shows the levels that can generally be evaluated within the same tool using common evaluation methods (Table 11-1).

Table 11-1. Evaluation Methods

METHODS	EVALUATION LEVELS			
	1 Reaction	2 Learning	3 Behavior	4 Results
Survey, questionnaire, individual or group interview	✓	✓	✓	✓
Action plan monitoring, action learning		✓	✓	✓
Work review, skill observation, behavior observation, action learning		✓	✓	
Case study, knowledge test, knowledge check, presentation, teach back		✓		
Request for validation			✓	✓
Key business and HR metrics				✓

Using Learner-Centered Items

A common complaint from learning and performance professionals is low-response rate and poor-quality responses on evaluation forms. One reason is that items tend to be phrased in terms of the trainer instead of from the perspective of the learner (Table 11-2).

Table 11-2. Trainer-Centered Versus Learner-Centered Items

Trainer-Centered Items	Learner-Centered Items
The course materials were well organized.	The course materials were easy to follow.
The facilitator demonstrated a good understanding of the content.	My learning was enhanced by the knowledge of the facilitator.
The activities were well developed.	The activities aided me in learning the concepts.

Making items learner centered shifts the focus from critiquing the program or the teacher to sharing a personal viewpoint or experience. In most cultures, this is more comfortable; it also provides an open door for honest and robust feedback.

Also ensure that all items are in common language, free of training jargon, and easy for your average person to understand. If training participants are struggling to understand the item, chances of obtaining meaningful data are small. For example, instead of asking about engagement, refer to involvement in the program. Instead of talking about learning objectives, refer to main ideas. Instead of referencing competencies, talk about skills required to perform their jobs.

Review your own evaluation questions to see if they are learner centered and phrased in plain language. You might consider testing them out on a few sample program participants to see what they think. If your questions fail either test, a simple rewording will likely increase both the quantity and quality of your future evaluation responses.

Sample Methods and Tools

This collection of sample methods and tools is provided to show you examples of how others have evaluated various types of common training programs.

These are only examples and templates for your reference. Evaluation tools should be customized to the program for which they are being used, considering what information is most useful to you and your organization or client.

Table 11-3. Sample 1: Electronic Participant Survey Completed Immediately After Training

Context: This one-hour asynchronous e-learning workplace safety course is required for employees annually. It is designed to teach and remind them to follow safety processes and procedures. Based on the program duration and the fact that it is required of all employees, only a few evaluation items are needed to gather information to confirm that the course is meeting its stated objectives.

	Strongly Disagree						Strongly Agree
1. The technology was easy to navigate.	1 ○	2 ○	3 ○	4 ○	5 ○	6 ○	7 ○
2. I am clear about how to follow safety processes and procedures.	1 ○	2 ○	3 ○	4 ○	5 ○	6 ○	7 ○
3. I have all the knowledge I need to be safe at work.	1 ○	2 ○	3 ○	4 ○	5 ○	6 ○	7 ○
4. I have all the equipment I need to be safe at work.	1 ○	2 ○	3 ○	4 ○	5 ○	6 ○	7 ○
5. I will remind my co-workers when they are not behaving in a safe manner.	1 ○	2 ○	3 ○	4 ○	5 ○	6 ○	7 ○

6. How can this safety course be improved?

Table 11-4. Sample 2: Electronic Participant Survey Completed Immediately After Training

Context: This two-hour customer service webinar is presented by a virtual, live instructor. It is designed to improve the job performance of customer service representatives.

	Strongly Disagree						Strongly Agree
	1	2	3	4	5	6	7
1. The instructor held my attention.	O	O	O	O	O	O	O
2. The content was easy for me to follow.	O	O	O	O	O	O	O
3. I was encouraged to participate throughout the webinar.	O	O	O	O	O	O	O
4. What I learned will help me do my job better.	O	O	O	O	O	O	O
5. I am clear about where I can find additional help after I get back to my job.	O	O	O	O	O	O	O
6. I am clear about what is expected of me on the job as a result of taking this course.	O	O	O	O	O	O	O

7. What is the FIRST thing that you plan to implement from what you have learned today?

8. How can the webinar be improved?

Table 11-5. Sample 3: Paper Participant Pulse Check Completed During Training

Context: This pulse check is administered at the end of day one of the Kirkpatrick certification program. The intent is to identify any issues that require attention or correction on day two of the program, or in subsequent program updates.

Kirkpatrick Day One Evaluation

Date and Location: _____

Instructions:

- For questions 1–3, please use the following rating scale:
  0 = strongly disagree   10 = strongly agree

- Please circle the appropriate rating to indicate the degree to which you agree with each statement.

- Please provide comments to explain your ratings.

- If your session had two facilitators, please fill in the key below and score each individually in question 3.
  Facilitator A: _____   Facilitator B: _____

Rating

Strongly disagree   Strongly agree

0 1 2 3 4 5 6 7 8 9 10   1. I took responsibility for being involved in today's session.
Comments:

0 1 2 3 4 5 6 7 8 9 10   2. The information in today's session is applicable to my work.
Comments:

A: 0 1 2 3 4 5 6 7 8 9 10   3. The presentation style of the facilitator contributed to my
B: 0 1 2 3 4 5 6 7 8 9 10   learning experience.
Comments:

4. Please provide any suggestions for change / improvement you may have for tomorrow and for future sessions of this program.

Table 11-6. Sample 4: Paper Participant Survey Completed Immediately After Training

Context: This survey is completed at the end of the two-day Kirkpatrick certification program.

Kirkpatrick Four Levels® Evaluation Certification Program

Participant Evaluation

Date and Location: _____

Instructions:

- For questions 1–5, please use the following rating scale:
  0 = strongly disagree   10 = strongly agree
- Please circle the appropriate rating to indicate the degree to which you agree with each statement.
- Please provide comments to explain your ratings.
- If your session had two facilitators, please fill in the key below and score each individually in question 3.
  Facilitator A: _____   Facilitator B: _____

Rating

Strongly disagree   Strongly agree

0 1 2 3 4 5 6 7 8 9 10   1. I took responsibility for being involved in this program.

Comments:

0 1 2 3 4 5 6 7 8 9 10   2. This program held my interest.

Comments:

A: 0 1 2 3 4 5 6 7 8 9 10   3. The presentation style of the facilitator contributed to
B: 0 1 2 3 4 5 6 7 8 9 10   my learning experience.

Comments:

0 1 2 3 4 5 6 7 8 9 10   4. The information in this program is applicable to my work.

Comments:

0 1 2 3 4 5 6 7 8 9 10   5. I would recommend this program to others.

Comments:

Table 11-6. Sample 4: Paper Participant Survey Completed Immediately After Training *(continued)*

Kirkpatrick Four Levels® Evaluation Certification Program

Participant Evaluation

Date and Location: _____

Instructions:

- For questions 6–8, please use the following rating scale:

1	2	3	4	5
None or very low level				Very high level

- Please circle the appropriate rating **before** the training and **now** (after the training).
- Please provide comments to explain your ratings.

Before the program   **After the program**

1 2 3 4 5	6. Knowledge of New World four-level program evaluation	1 2 3 4 5

Comments:

1 2 3 4 5	7. Confidence to evaluate programs to the appropriate level	1 2 3 4 5

Comments:

1 2 3 4 5	8. Commitment to evaluate programs to the appropriate level	1 2 3 4 5

Comments:

9. How can this program be improved?

10. Please share any additional comments you may have. If you authorize us to use your comments in Kirkpatrick marketing materials, please print your name and company name.

Table 11-7. Sample 5: Paper Instructor Survey Completed Immediately After Training

Context: This evaluation is completed by the instructor of the Kirkpatrick certification program. It taps into the less common data source of program instructors and eliminates the need for facilities-related questions on participant evaluation forms.

Kirkpatrick Certified Facilitator
Program Evaluation Form

Instructions: Complete this evaluation of the program you taught by saving a copy and typing into it.

Program name:

Facilitator name:

Location / client:

Date:

Please rate the knowledge of this group in the Kirkpatrick methodology at the beginning of the training program. Note the approximate percentage of participants at each level of proficiency, per your observations.

1 Little or no understanding	2 Basic understanding, but cannot demonstrate it	3 Understands and can demonstrate it with assistance	4 Can demonstrate without assistance	5 Can demonstrate and teach others to do it
%	%	%	%	%

Was the room set up per the instructions provided? — Yes / No
If no, what was wrong with the setup?

Did a manager, supervisor, or senior-level executive participate in the program? — Yes / No
If yes, who?

Instructions: Thinking about the course you just finished teaching, please indicate to what degree you agree with each statement using this rating scale:

1 = Strongly Disagree	2 = Disagree	3 = Agree	4 = Strongly Agree

Please provide comments along with your rating.

The participants were positive and receptive to the message. — Yes / No
Comments:

Overall, I am happy with how the program went. — Yes / No
Comments:

Please share any other comments you have about this program.
Comments:

Table 11-8. Sample 6: Participant Focus Group Question Set Facilitated Immediately After Training

Context: This participant focus group was conducted after the first offering of a new, week-long *Emerging Leader* program. Participants were advised prior to the program that they would be asked for detailed feedback and should take notes during class. This method is generally reserved for mission-critical programs, pilot programs, or when survey scores are significantly below standard.

What is your name and department?

What do you see as the major reasons you were asked to take this course?

We are going to review each of the program modules. Please share comments related to the notes you made during the program.

- Developing and sharing your vision
- Managing employee expectations
- Building strong teams
- Performance management
- Driving to the end: business results

What if anything was a hindrance to your experience?

How do you plan to apply what you learned?

What additional help would you like in order to be successful?

What outcomes are you expecting to see from your efforts?

Table 11-9. Sample 7: Paper Supervisor Checklist Completed After Training

Context: This is a checklist that supervisors use while listening to customer service calls to rate customer service representative (CSR) performance after CSRs have completed training.

Rating Scale

1 = Effective use of targeted behavior

2 = Moderately effective use of targeted behavior

3 = Ineffective use of targeted behavior

Coaching comments may include specific observations that support the rating, as well as coaching notes to help the associate to be more effective.

Target Behavior	Rating	Coaching Comments
CSR made good initial connection with the callers' needs to create a rational exchange.		
CSR used relevant, open-ended questions to gather initial information about the callers' needs.		
CSR asked follow-up questions to gain further clarification of the callers' needs.		
CSR presented relevant possible solutions to the callers' concerns.		
CSR offered ongoing support to address the callers' needs while considering the best interests of the company.		
CSR closed the meeting with a clear course of problem resolution.		

Table 11-10. Sample 8: Electronic Supervisor Survey Completed on a Delayed Basis After Training

Context: This survey was completed by supervisors a few months after their direct reports participated in a three-week customer service program. This mission-critical program has specific performance expectations designed to make a significant contribution to the organization's strategy; these expectations were outlined for supervisors prior to the program.

	Strongly Disagree						Strongly Agree
	1	2	3	4	5	6	7
1. After the course, I spent adequate time with my employees to discuss how they will use their new skills in their jobs.	O	O	O	O	O	O	O
2. My employees have adequate resources on the job to successfully apply what they learned in training.	O	O	O	O	O	O	O
3. My employees have successfully applied the knowledge/skills learned in this course to their jobs.	O	O	O	O	O	O	O

4. Rate your level of agreement with this statement: Each item listed below is a significant factor that contributed to my employees successfully applying what they learned.

	1	2	3	4	5	6	7
• The program itself	O	O	O	O	O	O	O
• Post-program help from course instructors	O	O	O	O	O	O	O
• Customer service community of practice	O	O	O	O	O	O	O
• Support from their peers	O	O	O	O	O	O	O
• Coaching from me as their immediate supervisor	O	O	O	O	O	O	O
• Additional on-the-job training	O	O	O	O	O	O	O
• Referring back to the program materials	O	O	O	O	O	O	O
• Job aids provided by the instructor	O	O	O	O	O	O	O
• Performance incentives	O	O	O	O	O	O	O

Table 11-10. Sample 8: Electronic Supervisor Survey Completed on a Delayed Basis After Training *(continued)*

	Strongly Disagree						Strongly Agree
	1	2	3	4	5	6	7

5. Here are factors that often cause employees to struggle with their performance. Rate your level of agreement that these factors are present.

	1	2	3	4	5	6	7
• What they learned is not useful in their jobs.	O	O	O	O	O	O	O
• They do not have the necessary skills.	O	O	O	O	O	O	O
• They were not sure what was expected of them on the job.	O	O	O	O	O	O	O
• They do not have the necessary resources.	O	O	O	O	O	O	O
• I did not provide them with adequate supervisory support.	O	O	O	O	O	O	O
• They were discouraged from using their training.	O	O	O	O	O	O	O
• They didn't remember what they learned.	O	O	O	O	O	O	O
• They had too many other things to do.	O	O	O	O	O	O	O
• They tried and it didn't work.	O	O	O	O	O	O	O
• There was not an adequate system of accountability to ensure application.	O	O	O	O	O	O	O

6. I am already seeing positive results from my employee(s) as a result of this program.

1	2	3	4	5	6	7
O	◉	O	O	O	O	O

Comments:

7. Those who have successfully applied what they learned have positively impacted the following areas (check all that apply):

❑ One-call resolution	❑ Unsolicited customer referrals	❑ Brand perception
❑ Customer satisfaction	❑ Compliment/complaint ratio	❑ Employee satisfaction
❑ Call resolution time	❑ Customer retention	

8. What would increase on-the-job application?

Table 11-11. Sample 9: Participant Interview Question Set for Use on a Delayed Basis After Training

Context: This tool was used during a major sales training initiative long enough after training that outcomes had occurred. The goal was to gather testimonials, success factors, and barriers to success, supporting other data already collected to incorporate into the final program presentation and report.

1. How are you currently using what you learned during the sales training initiative?

2. What positive outcomes are you seeing as a result of what you are doing? *(Referring to the examples participants provide in #1, prompt them to share any success stories for themselves, the company, clients, etc. When appropriate, probe for historical comparisons of what was occurring before training and now.)*

3. To what can you attribute that success? *(Here you are asking participants to identify the success factors that supported their performance and yielded the subsequent results.)*

4. If you are not using the skills you learned during training, what are the reasons?

Table 11-12. Sample 10: Electronic Supervisor Request for Validation on a Delayed Basis After Training

Context: This simple note was emailed to supervisors of participants several months after a one-week decision-making program was conducted. This method does not require a high response rate to capture powerful testimonials to include in the final program report. It does, however, require that the supervisors were actively involved in the program and keyed in to what performance and results they should be seeing from their direct reports.

Dear Mitchell,

Many of your junior leaders completed the *Critical Decision-Making* program six months ago. Based on the significant investment in this program, we would like to know your views on its success.

Could you or someone on your team provide a testimonial related to the value of this program? If so, please either email me the story, or simply call me at your convenience. It should only take about five minutes of your time.

Here are examples of the types of stories past programs have generated:

- Before training, Susan would defer to me whenever there was a decision to be made. Now, she gathers all the facts on her own and comes to me with them, and a proposal for the action she recommends. She has built stronger customer relationships as a result, and her sales are up this quarter.

- After training, William was faced with deciding whether or not to launch a product that still had some bugs but was highly demanded in the market. Using the decision-making process, he and a team found a compromise in which the product was delayed by two weeks but launched only with issues that would not be experienced by a customer before they could also be resolved. Using the process and working together, they got the product to market as quickly as possible, and helped us keep our reputation as a trusted supplier.

Thank you for your time. Feel free to contact me if you have any questions or other comments related to this program.

Best Regards,

Jim Kirkpatrick

Item Library for Use Immediately Following Training

A library of sample evaluation items for use immediately following training is provided as the basis to help you to build your own evaluation form or tool. These are truly sample items; there is no one correct question or question set that will always work for you.

Use these items to customize evaluation tools that meet your individual needs and criteria. Keep usefulness and credibility in mind as you select the exact items and questions. A word of caution about benchmarking: only use this as a reason to include a specific item if it is truly relevant to the program and will give you usable data. Don't include questions simply because they are being benchmarked.

The following items are most commonly incorporated into a written survey, but they also can be used for interviews and focus groups. To convert the rating scale items for interview or focus group use, just add "to what degree" to the beginning and modify the wording slightly to convert them into questions.

LEVEL 1: REACTION

Engagement

Rating Scale Items

> The class environment helped me to learn.
>
> My participation was encouraged by the facilitator.
>
> This program held my interest.

Open-ended Question

> Was there anything about your experience that interfered with your learning? If so, what?

Relevance

Rating Scale Items

> What I learned from this course will help me on the job.
>
> During class, we discussed how to apply what we learned.
>
> I am clear about what is expected of me when I get back to my job.

Open-ended Questions

> What material did you find to be the most relevant to your job?
>
> What material was a waste of time?

Customer Satisfaction

Rating Scale Items

> I received helpful information prior to the program.
>
> I will recommend this program to my co-workers.

Open-ended Question
> How could this program be improved?

LEVEL 2: LEARNING

Knowledge

Knowledge is measured primarily with formative exercises during the session or a quiz near the end.

Open-ended Question
> What are the major concepts that you learned during this session?

Skills

Skill is measured with activities and demonstrations during the session that show that participants can perform the skill. Unless the skill relates to writing, it is rare to evaluate skill in a post-program evaluation.

Attitude

Rating Scale Item
> I believe it will be worthwhile for me to apply what I learned.

Open-ended Question
> What is the importance of applying what you learned on the job?

Confidence

Rating Scale Items
> I feel confident about applying what I learned back on the job.
>
> I anticipate that I will receive the necessary support to successfully apply what I learned.
>
> My confidence is not high because:
> a) I do not have the necessary knowledge and skills.
> b) I do not have a clear picture of what is expected of me.
> c) I have other, higher priorities.
> d) I do not have the necessary resources to apply what I learned.
> e) I do not have the support to apply what I learned.
> f) I don't think what I learned will work.
> g) There is not an adequate system of accountability to ensure application of what I learned.
> h) Other (please explain):

Open-ended Questions

What additional support will you need to implement what you learned?

What barriers do you anticipate that could limit your success at applying what you learned?

Please comment on how confident you feel about applying what you have just learned on the job.

Commitment

Rating Scale Item

I am committed to applying what I learned to my work.

Open-ended Questions

How do you plan to apply what you learned when you get back to your job?

What is the first thing that you plan to apply from what you have learned today?

PREDICTIVE LEVEL 4: RESULTS

Rating Scale Item

I believe I will see a positive impact if I consistently apply what I learned.

Open-ended Questions

What initial successes will likely occur as you apply what you learned?

What specific outcomes are you hoping to achieve as a result of your efforts?

Item Library for Delayed Use After Training

This library of sample evaluation items for use on a delayed basis following training is provided as the basis to help you to build your own evaluation form or tool. A commonly asked question is when to perform the delayed evaluation. The best timing is after the required drivers are engaged, and participants have had the opportunity to apply the new skills on the job. The timing will vary depending upon the type of knowledge or skills being taught.

Often, training professionals call this their "90-day survey." A better approach is to consider when it is appropriate to gather data, and with what methods or tools. As with the first item library, these are truly sample items; there is no single set of questions to use for all training. Use these items in the same way as the first item library to customize evaluation tools that meet your individual needs and criteria.

DELAYED LEVEL 1: REACTION

Relevance

Rating Scale Items

I have had occasion in my job to use what I learned in this course.

The information provided in this course is applicable to my job.

Open-ended Questions

What information from this course has been the most relevant to your job?

Was there any information in this course that is NOT relevant to your job? If so, what?

What information should be added to this course to make it more relevant to your work?

Customer Satisfaction

Rating Scale Item

Looking back, taking this course was a good use of my time.

Open-ended Questions

Looking back, how could this program have been improved?

Looking back, what would you change about this course?

DELAYED LEVEL 2 LEARNING

If you performed evaluation well during and immediately following training, it is seldom necessary to reevaluate knowledge and skill. However, if these were not adequately performed and the actual knowledge and skill of program graduates is in question, you could ask some content-related questions.

LEVEL 3: BEHAVIOR

Rating Scale Items

I have successfully applied on the job what I learned in training.

I have been able to apply on the job what I learned in class.

INSTRUCTIONS: Using this rating scale, circle the rating that best describes your current level of on-the-job application for each listed behavior (Table 11-13).

Table 11-13. Level 3: Behavior Rating Scale

| 1– Little or no application |
| 2– Mild degree of application |
| 3– Moderate degree of application |
| 4– Strong degree of application |
| 5– Very strong degree of application, and desire to help others do the same |

Insert behavioral objective #1	1	2	3	4	5
Insert behavioral objective #2	1	2	3	4	5
Insert behavioral objective #3	1	2	3	4	5

I have applied what I learned to my work.

If you circled 5 or above (on a 7-point scale) for the previous question, rate the contribution of each of the following factors to your effective performance (Table 11-14).

If you circled 4 or below, please indicate the reasons (check all that apply):

☐ I do not have the necessary knowledge and skills.

☐ I do not have a clear picture of what is expected of me.

☐ I have other, higher priorities.

☐ I do not have the necessary resources to apply what I learned.

☐ I do not have the support to apply what I learned.

☐ The training didn't give me the confidence to apply what I learned.

☐ I don't think what I learned will work.

☐ There is not an adequate system of accountability to ensure application of what I learned.

☐ Other (please explain):

Open-ended Questions

How have you used what you learned in training on the job?

Describe any challenges you are experiencing in applying what you learned to your work, and possible solutions to overcome them.

Table 11-14. Rating Scale for Contributing Factors

Contributing Factor	Rating			
The course itself	Not at all	Low	Medium	High
Coaching from my supervisor	Not at all	Low	Medium	High
Support and/or encouragement	Not at all	Low	Medium	High
Effective system of accountability or monitoring	Not at all	Low	Medium	High
Belief that it would help me to be more effective in my work	Not at all	Low	Medium	High
Ongoing training I have received after the initial class	Not at all	Low	Medium	High
Payment of bonus or other incentives	Not at all	Low	Medium	High
Community of practice or other peer support	Not at all	Low	Medium	High
Job aids	Not at all	Low	Medium	High
Other (please specify):	Not at all	Low	Medium	High

Required Drivers

Rating Scale Items

My supervisor and I set expectations for this training before the class.

My supervisor and I determined how I would apply what I learned after training.

I have received support in order to apply what I learned successfully.

Open-ended Questions

What else do you need to successfully perform the skills you learned in this program while on the job?

What has helped you to implement what you learned?

LEVEL 4: RESULTS TRAINING AND EVALUATION

Leading Indicators

Rating Scale Items

I am already seeing positive results from the training.

I have seen an impact in the following areas as a result of applying what I learned (check all that apply):

- ☐ Increased quality
- ☐ Improved productivity
- ☐ Increased personal confidence
- ☐ Increased customer satisfaction
- ☐ Stronger relationships with my clients
- ☐ More respect from my peers
- ☐ Better organization in my work
- ☐ Other (please explain):

Open-ended Questions

What early signs of success have you noticed from your efforts?

Please give an example of a positive outcome you have experienced since attending this training.

Desired Results

Rating Scale Items

This program has positively impacted my department.

My efforts have contributed to the mission of this organization.

Open-ended Questions

What impact is this program having on the organization as a whole?

How has your participation in this program benefited the company?

Summary

Many training professionals ask for "the form"; however, a standardized evaluation form that works in all circumstances does not exist. Rather, evaluation forms and tools are built based on program needs.

Instead of viewing the four levels as mutually exclusive, a Blended Evaluation approach, or one in which multiple levels are evaluated simultaneously, should be used. This approach maximizes evaluation resources and prevents survey fatigue.

When designing an evaluation tool, use questions that are learner-centered, or phrased from the perspective of the learner's experience in the program, rather than putting them in the position of directly rating the performance of others.

Use usefulness and credibility as your guide for what types of information you gather in your evaluation; don't trust one-size-fits-all approaches and don't be overly concerned with benchmarks used by others. Keep a close eye on the length of the evaluation related to the importance of the initiative to the organization.

Using a Blended Evaluation approach with a strategically selected learner-centered item set will maximize response rate and usable data.

PART 3

Data Analysis and Reporting Basics

Part 3 of this book provides practical, nonscientific methods for analyzing data, making good decisions to guide program process, and reporting findings and outcomes in plain language for all stakeholder groups.

Data analysis and reporting is an ongoing process that occurs throughout program implementation, not a discrete activity that occurs at the end of the process. Analyzing data and acting upon it provides the opportunity to influence the course of a program and maximize its outcomes and value. Simply reporting what happened in arrears only serves to use resources, not contribute to program value.

In the same way that many people are searching for the magical, one-size-fits-all evaluation form, many are also seeking the standardized final report of program outcomes. Quite simply, it does not exist. Rather, chapter 15 provides guidelines to assist you in creating a straightforward and professional final report that will show stakeholders what is important to them. Examples of how the advice has been operationalized by other organizations are provided in Part 4 of this book.

Part 3 also contains perspectives from other industry experts related to maximizing program value and sharing the story with others. We believe that you will find their advice helpful in honing your own training evaluation strategy.

This section ends with a collection of the most common evaluation pitfalls that hopefully by this point in the book you are well equipped to avoid. Chapter 16 could be used as an informal quiz to assess where you and your organization are today with your training evaluation practices.

CHAPTER 12

Making Data-Based Decisions

Employing the ideas presented so far will allow you to gather a robust data set containing both quantitative and qualitative items. The next step is to analyze the data and take appropriate action. If you are following the recommendations, you already realize that you do not want to wait until after the program is complete to gather data, and then wait further to analyze it and see what happened. Instead, you want to gather and analyze data along the way so that instead of measuring what happened, you can influence what happens and maximize current and future program results.

As you begin to amass a sizable data set during implementation, keep in mind the goals of the program and the plan that was set at the beginning. Be discerning as to which data are useful to you and will create credibility in the eyes of your stakeholders.

A key data analysis concept to keep in mind is "signal-to-noise ratio." Imagine people huddled around an old Victrola radio in the 1940s to hear the voice of Franklin Roosevelt or Winston Churchill. Picture a dad with his ear to the speaker, gently moving the dial to get the clearest signal with the least possible background noise and static.

In our current age of information, the signal-to-noise ratio is high because there is such easy access to a large amount of evaluation data, mostly at Levels 1 and 2. The key is to filter out the noise, the data that are neither useful to you nor important to your stakeholders, so that you are left with just the signal, the data that assist you in making good decisions and showing the value of the initiative to your stakeholders.

Three Key Data Analysis Questions

As you gather formative and summative data during program implementation, ask and get answers to these three key questions:

1. Does . . . meet expectations?
2. If not, why not?
3. If so, why?

Does . . . Meet Expectations?

The first question to ask is, "Does the level of . . . meet expectations?" This question can and should be asked when evaluating the data collected at each of the four levels (Table 12-1).

For Levels 1 and 2, the range of acceptable expectations is largely determined by the training department. For Level 3, critical behaviors are expected to be performed consistently, by definition. Expectations for program outcomes in the form of leading indicators, shown in Level 4, should have been defined during the program planning phase, and they are unique to each program.

Organizations that wish to benchmark as a way to know if their performance is acceptable can consider internal benchmarking and competing against themselves for continual improvement. It is also possible that specific target metrics cannot realistically be determined up front. In that case, it would be prudent to make an educated guess and then use some pilot data to fine-tune expectations.

There is no need to make this complicated. For each level, you are simply asking yourself if the data you collected indicates that you have or have not met the requirements for each component.

If Not, Why Not?

As the program progresses and you are analyzing related data, it is likely that for at least one component, the outcomes will not meet the expectation. If they do not, you need to identify and correct the issue before the targeted results are jeopardized.

Data analysis resources should be focused on Levels 3 and 4, much the same way as overall program resources should be allocated to favor these more important levels. However, this process also works well for Levels 1 and 2.

Data Analysis During a Training Program

Streamline analysis at Levels 1 and 2 by having trainers conduct analysis formatively, as they teach the program. For example, they can mentally assess if the level of interaction during the program meets their expectations, based on their experience. If it doesn't, they can conduct a pulse check, in which they stop teaching momentarily and ask the class open-ended questions to determine if there is something inhibiting participation. For example, "I see some confused looks out there. What thoughts do you have?"

Table 12-1. Data Analysis Questions

LEVEL 1: REACTION

Does participant **engagement** during the program meet expectations?

Does **relevance** of the program to participant job responsibilities meet expectations?

Does participant **satisfaction** with the program meet expectations?

LEVEL 2: LEARNING

Does participant **knowledge** obtained / demonstrated during the program meet expectations?

Does participant **skill** demonstrated during the program meet expectations?

Does participant **attitude** about performing new skills on the job meet expectations?

Does participant **confidence** to apply knowledge and skills on the job meet expectations?

Does participant **commitment** to apply knowledge and skills on the job meet expectations?

LEVEL 3: BEHAVIOR

Does performance of (*insert **critical behavior***) on the job meet expectations?

Does level of on-the-job learning meet expectations?

Required Drivers

Does the quality and amount of performance monitoring meet expectations?

Does reinforcement of critical behaviors meet expectations?

Does encouragement to perform critical behaviors meet expectations?

Does the alignment of reward systems and performance of critical behaviors meet expectations?

LEVEL 4: RESULTS

Does movement of (*insert **leading indicator***) meet expectations?

Does movement of (*insert **desired outcomes***) meet expectations?

Data Analysis After the Training Program

After training, the data analysis process continues and becomes arguably more critical as on-the-job performance is monitored for acceptable levels. When monitoring Level 3, it is uncommon for a single variable to cause substandard performance. As a learning and performance consultant, at this stage you can help uncover barriers to performance in the workplace and participate in creating solutions.

This punctuates the importance of creating a good post-training plan; if you do not have monitoring methods lined up in advance, getting and responding to the data will be awkward, or even impossible.

Shown here are a few examples of how to identify possible root causes of substandard data (Table 12-2).

Depending upon the culture in your organization, being a learning and performance consultant may require some courage. Some stakeholders may be less than enthusiastic to hear your bad news as you share that the implementation is off track, even if you have suggestions to get it back on target. Some managers or supervisors may tell you to "go back to where you belong."

When Wendy worked for a large corporation, a sales manager once asked her what she was doing poking around trying to get sales statistics by sales rep. This is not uncommon, and if your organization does not already have a culture of business partnership, it will likely happen to you, too.

It is important to keep in mind that it is your job to first seek the truth through assessment and analysis. Then, you need to speak the truth about the suspected root causes and recommended interventions to remedy the situation. In the long run, truth leads to trust.

Linda Hainlen, a former training director for a large healthcare organization, reported that her team gained the most respect from stakeholders when they shared the identified barriers to implementation, and then what they did to resolve them. She said that if all she did was paint a picture that everything was perfect, they wouldn't really believe that was the case and would not trust her as much.

Timely, proactive data analysis and response maximize program outcomes because issues are revealed and addressed when there is still time to fix them. There is so much less value in only measuring and reporting what happened after an initiative is over; this only serves to document the program outcomes, and best case, to generate ideas to enhance future initiatives.

If So, Why?

Ideally, when you probe to find out if various program outcomes are meeting expectations, sometimes the answer will be "yes." If this is the case, study these pockets of success to see if they can be propagated, expanded, publicized, or celebrated.

Table 12-2. Root Cause Identification Tactics

ALL LEVELS

Include conditional questions in surveys and interviews.
    (e.g., If you rated this item 3 or below, please indicate the reason(s).)

Ask program instructors for their input.

Ask managers and supervisors of the training graduates for their observations and input.

Drill down into data to determine if the problem is global or isolated.
    (e.g., Is the issue specific to one department, geography, or job title?)

Conduct training participant interviews or a focus group and ask open-ended questions. When indicated, ask follow-on questions.

LEVEL 1: REACTION	LEVEL 2: LEARNING

Integrate formative evaluation into the training program.

LEVEL 3: BEHAVIOR

Observe on-the-job behavior and watch for obstructions to critical behaviors and required drivers.

Survey or interview training graduates and their supervisors, customers, co-workers and/or direct reports and ask them why they think that critical behaviors and required drivers are not occurring reliably. Ask them what would make them occur.

LEVEL 4: RESULTS

Survey or interview training graduates and their supervisors, customers, co-workers and/or direct reports and ask them why they think that leading indicators and/or desired results are not moving in the right direction. Ask them what behaviors or circumstances would make them move in the right direction.

Propagating Positive Findings From the Training Program

During the training program, the instructor may experience an enthusiastic, engaged participant group. If so, it might be appropriate to say, "All of a sudden the room seems to have come to life. Would you kindly share where you think that might have come from?"

These Levels 1 and 2 findings can be reviewed by the training department to continually improve the quality of future programs. As an added bonus, little or no time on the part of training participants and business stakeholders is required for this analysis at Levels 1 and 2.

Propagating Positive Findings on the Job

Sometimes program success is linked directly to certain training graduates who are performing better than others on the job. We call these individuals Bright Lights™ because they embody success and inspire and lead the way for others. Identify these Bright Lights, capture what they do that is successful, and then identify what factors have contributed to their success. Chapter 13 provides a more detailed method for leveraging pockets of high performance.

Much like with barriers to implementation, successful implementation is typically the result of multiple success factors, rather than just one. When you are trying to capture these success factors, do not rely on surveys alone. Surveys may indicate where to begin looking for success factors, but ultimately, to get a complete picture, you will need to talk to training graduates, their supervisors, and possibly their peers and customers. Refer to chapter 11 for tools and sample questions.

Once these success factors have been identified, you may be able to add them to a learning and performance architecture as items that tend to drive success in your organization. This package can then both predict and maximize future mission-critical program outcomes.

Summary

Do not wait until after a program is complete to gather data, and then wait further to analyze it and see what happened. Instead, you want to gather and analyze data along the way so that instead of measuring what happened, you can influence what happens and maximize current and future program results.

As you begin to amass a sizable data set during implementation, be discerning as to which data are useful to you and will create credibility in the eyes of your stakeholders. As you analyze the useful data, ask yourself the three key data analysis questions:

1. Does . . . meet expectations?
2. If not, why not?
3. If so, why?

First, compare current data to predetermined expectations. If data indicate that expectations are not being met, search for the causes of the problems, address and correct them, and get the program back on track. If outcomes are meeting expectations, communicate early successes to keep everyone motivated toward the ultimate goal, and consider how to leverage success factors in future programs.

Systematic data analysis and response will increase not only the success of the current program, but also provide the tools to maximize outcomes of all future mission-critical initiatives.

CHAPTER 13

Using the Success Case Method to Drive Performance and Results

Robert O. Brinkerhoff and Timothy P. Mooney

The Success Case Method (SCM) measures and evaluates training accurately, simply, and quickly, in a way that is both extremely credible and compelling. Results derived through SCM application are actionable. Through strategic and constructive use of evaluation findings, trainers and their outcomes can be more effective and successful.

There is an additional strategic outcome that the SCM helps to achieve. For decades, training and development professionals have recognized that manager support for training is absolutely vital to success. When managers support training and learners, it works. When they don't, it does not. The SCM provides a clear, data-based business case for managers to support training. With the SCM, they can be shown specific actions they can take to reinforce learning and performance, actions tied directly to bottom-line results and economic payoff to them and their organizations. We can simply show managers the data so that they can look at the facts and make a business decision.

The SCM uncovers and pinpoints the factors that make or break training success. Then, it shows how these factors can be managed more effectively so that more learning turns into worthwhile performance in the future. It is aimed directly at helping leaders in an organization discover their organization's "learning disabilities" and then figure out what needs to be done to overcome them. Over time, the SCM helps

This chapter is adapted from "The Success Case Method: Using Evaluation to Improve Training Value and Impact," by Robert O. Brinkerhoff and Timothy P. Mooney, which appeared as chapter 9 in the ASTD Handbook of Measuring and Evaluating Training, *edited by Patricia Pulliam Phillips (Alexandria, VA: ASTD Press, 2010).*

an organization become better and better at turning an ounce of training investment into a pound of effective performance.

Defining Success

Some reasons for conducting training include promoting advancement and career fulfillment, to avoid legal exposure, to meet regulatory requirements to provide certain training, or simply to offer training because it is perceived as a staff benefit, which may help recruitment and personnel retention. These sorts of training do not necessarily require applying skills to produce value; thus, they are not the focus of typical SCM applications.

Most kinds of training conducted in organizations currently, however, are based on the belief that some employees need certain knowledge or skills to perform their jobs correctly or to improve their current job performance, and that the required knowledge and skills can be delivered through training. After attending training, trainees are then supposed to return to their jobs and correctly use the training-acquired skills to perform in their jobs. Eventually, so goes this rationale, the company will benefit from the application of these skills through increased revenues, higher-quality products, more productive employees, increased output, decreased scrap rates, and so forth.

Note that the benefit to the organization derives not from what was learned but from what actually gets used—that is, value doesn't come from exposure to the training or the acquisition of new capabilities. Instead, value comes from the changes in performance that the training eventually leads to. Impact and value are achieved only when the training actually gets used to improve or sustain job performance. Thus, for the majority of training programs, training success is defined as application of training-acquired capabilities leading to improved performance and job results.

Training Evaluation Realities

Two realities about training programs must be recognized and effectively dealt with because they dramatically influence the way trainers should think about and conduct training evaluation. The first reality is that training results are predictable, and the second reality is that training alone never works.

Reality One: Predictable Results

Training programs typically produce reliable—and unfortunately marginal—results. The results that some trainees achieve may not be at all marginal, but over a large group of trainees, overall results are typically mediocre at best. Some people use their learning in ways that get great results for their organizations. Others do not use their learning at all. The majority may try some parts of it, notice little if any changes or results, and eventually go back to the ways they were doing things before. The good news is that the few who actually use their training in effective on-the-job applications often achieve highly valuable results. For example, one manager used her training to help land a $500 million sale, a result that would not have been achieved had she not participated in the training. In another instance, a senior leader used his training to increase operating income for his business division by more than $1.87 million. These are dramatic and exceptionally valuable results; we have documented many more less dramatic outcomes that were nonetheless significant and noteworthy.

So, the problem is not that training does not work at all; it is just that it does not work frequently enough with enough trainees. In most cases, a typical training program produces only a few quite successful trainees who achieve these great results. Similarly, there is typically a small (but sometimes not so small) percentage of people who, for one reason or another, were not able to use their training at all, or didn't even try to. The bulk of trainees are distributed between these extremes.

Making a Business Case to "Grow" Impact
A key principle of the SCM is that we can learn a lot from inquiring about the experience of these extreme groups. An SCM study can tell us, for example, how much good a training initiative generated when the learning it produced is used in on-the-job performance. If it generated a great deal of good, such as when some trainees use their learning in a way that leads to highly valuable business results, then we know that the training had great potential for a high return on investment. When we find that the training produced really worthwhile results, but that it worked this well with only a small number of trainees, then we can construct a defensible business case for investing time and resources to extend the good results to more people.

Tyranny of the Mean
Typical quantitative evaluation approaches are based on reductionist statistical procedures, such as calculating a mean or "average" effect. But, because training typically only helps achieve worthwhile results for a small proportion of the trainees, on average, training will always be calculated to be mediocre. When we have a range of effects, those at the high end will be offset by those at the low end when we calculate a mean score. Assume for purposes of illustration that we have two different training programs, A and B. In training program A, assume further that we had an evenly split distribution of impact such that one half of the trainees did extremely well with their

training, using it to improve their performance and achieve worthy results, while the other half did not use their learning at all. If we added these two halves of the distribution together and divided by the total number of trainees, as we would do in determining a mean score, then the training would look to have, overall, mediocre results. Assume that program B worked equally well with virtually all of the trainees, but was mediocre in that none of the trainees used their learning in useful ways, although none failed to use their learning either. That is, they all used it, but all in a mediocre way.

When we calculate the mean impact of program B, it will appear to have had exactly the same results as program A. In reality, however, these two programs represent two different strategic scenarios. In the case of program A, it has great potential because it produced excellent results, although for only half of the trainees. It is clearly a powerful intervention, although for some reason only half of the participants were able to get these results. Program B, however, has little to no promise, as it works well with virtually no one. It is probably not worth keeping.

This "tyranny of the mean" effect is very powerful and at the same time very dangerous. It probably explains why, on average, most training programs have, over the years, been assessed as having only mediocre effects. While it is true that most training does not work well, some programs do work well with some of the people, and this represents their great potential for being leveraged for even greater results.

The SCM avoids this tyranny of the mean effect by intentionally separating out the trainees who used their training, then aiming to discover what value those applications of the training produced. So, the SCM does not ask, "On average, how well is the training working?" (We already know the answer to that question: not very well). Instead, the SCM asks, "When the training works (is used), what good does it do?"

Reality Two: Training Alone Never Works

Training and performance improvement practitioners wanting to evaluate their success have struggled for decades with the seemingly intractable issue that "other factors" are always at work with training. In a sales training program, for example, we might see an increase in sales, or we might not. How do we know it was the training that led to increased sales or the lack thereof? Maybe it was some other factor, such as a change in the market, a new incentive to sell more, or something else. Training alone does not produce results. There are always a number of nontraining factors that enable or impede successful results from the training. Supervisory support, incentives, opportunities to try out learning, and the timing of the training, to name a few, are examples of the sorts of nontraining or performance system factors that determine whether and how well training works to improve performance.

A corollary of this reality is the fact that when training works or does not work, it is most often the case that the nontraining factors account for more of the success or failure than features and elements of the training intervention or program itself.

This second reality of training evaluation strongly suggests that most—potentially 80 percent or more—of the failures of training to achieve results are *not* caused by flawed training interventions, but rather by contextual and performance system factors that were not aligned with or were otherwise at odds with the intended performance outcomes of the training. Thus, when we evaluate "training" impact, we are most often, in reality, evaluating an organization's performance management system.

This fact is nothing new. We have known for years that the major reason for the failure of training to achieve impact is that training readiness and performance support factors were never adequately developed or implemented. Most evaluation models and methods have attempted to cope with this reality by trying to isolate the training-related causes.

In common practice, the way that this reality is often dealt with is to avoid it and evaluate only the training itself, asking whether it appeared to be useful in the eyes of participants, and sometimes going so far as to measure whether people actually learned anything. But going beyond this to measure application of learning has typically not been very productive. First, surveys of learning application produce discouraging results, showing quite predictably that most trainees have not applied or sustained use of their learning. Second, when we discover that most trainees are not using their learning in sustained performance, there is little we do with this information because trying to improve the rate of application by improving the training program itself will not yield concomitant improvements in applying learning on the job.

The SCM, on the other hand, makes no attempt to "parcel out" or otherwise isolate the training-related causes or to make any training-specific causal claims.

Instead, we leverage the fact that training never works alone or in a vacuum. We seek in an SCM study to identify all of the major factors that helped or hindered the achievement of worthwhile performance results from training so that we can build on and leverage this knowledge into recommendations for increasing performance in later iterations of training efforts. We discovered in an evaluation of a training program for financial advisors, for instance, that almost all new advisors who were successful in applying their learning and getting good financial results had also made use of additional resources that helped them practice new emotional competence skills on the job. We also discovered that nearly all of the successful advisors sought and received feedback from a manager or peer. We concluded that the training was very unlikely to get any positive results without such additional interactions. This led, in turn, to recommendations to future trainees and their managers to be sure to provide time and opportunity for such assistance, because without it, the training was likely to be ineffective and wasted.

Leveraging the Two Realities

The SCM begins with a survey to determine the general distribution of those training graduates who are using their learning to get worthwhile results and those who are most likely not having such success. In the second stage of an SCM study, we conduct in-depth interviews with a few of these successes and nonsuccesses—just enough of them to be sure we have valid and trustworthy data. The purpose of the interviews is twofold. First, we seek to understand, analyze, and document the actual scope and value of the good results that the apparently successful people have claimed from the survey phase. This allows us to verify the actual rate of success, and also to gauge its value. In an SCM study of sales representatives, for example, we were able to determine that the actual rate of success was about 17 percent; that is, 17 percent of the trainees who completed the training used their new learning in sustained and improved performance. Further, we could determine that the results they achieved were of a known value; in this example, the typical results were worth about $25,000 per quarter in increased profits from sales of products with more favorable margins.

This first part of the SCM, identifying the quantitative distribution of extremes of success, is typically accomplished with a brief survey. That is, we usually conduct a simple survey of all the participants in a training program and ask them, through a few carefully constructed items, the extent to which they have used their learning to get any worthwhile results. Although a survey is often used, it is not always necessary. It may be possible to identify potential success cases by reviewing usage records and reports, accessing performance data, or simply by asking people—tapping into the "information grapevine" of the organization.

A survey is most often used, however, because it provides the additional advantage of being able to extrapolate results to get quantitative estimates of the proportions of people who report using or not using their training. Also, when careful sampling methods are used, probability estimates of the nature and scope of success can also be determined.

Second, in the interview phase, we probe deeply to identify and understand the training-related factors (using certain parts of the training or particular tools taught in the training, for instance) and performance-system factors (supervisory assistance, incentives, feedback, and so forth) that differentiated nonsuccesses from successes. We know that when the training works, it is likely that it has been supported by and in interaction with certain replicable contextual factors. Knowing what these factors are enables us to make recommendations for helping subsequent trainees and later versions of the training initiative achieve better results.

Putting information from both of these SCM phases together creates highly powerful and useful information. First, we know what rate of success the training had, and the value of that rate in terms of the nature of the results that successful trainees were able to achieve using their learning. This lets us extrapolate the *unrealized* value of the training initiative—the value that was "left on the table" by the program due to its rate of nonsuccess instances.

A typical distribution of training results shows a relatively small proportion of trainees who used their learning and achieved positive results and a larger proportion who did not achieve worthwhile results (Figure 13-1). Added to this is a notation of the proportion of the distribution that represents a positive return on the training investment (ROI), as well as the proportion that had a negative return. The area above the darker and solid-line arrow shows that the trainees in this portion of the distribution achieved a positive ROI; we assume for purposes of this illustration that the value of the positive results in this portion of the distribution is indeed greater than the cost of providing and supporting the training for the people depicted in this portion. That is, whatever was spent to train the people who are represented in the solid-line area of the distribution was exceeded by the value of the results they achieved. However, everything to the left of this dividing line represents a loss or negative ROI. These people in the area above the dotted line were trained but did not use their learning in ways that led to positive results.

Figure 13-1. Typical Training Results Distribution

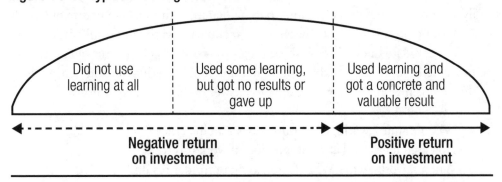

© Robert O. Brinkerhoff and Timothy P. Mooney

Given this, the larger the area of the distribution above the solid-line arrow, the greater the ROI. If we were to double, for example, the number of people who used their learning and achieved positive results, this clearly would dramatically increase the overall ROI of the training because the costs for training all of the people in the distribution are roughly the same for each individual. Or, looked at another way, the distribution to the left of the solid-line arrow area represents the unrealized value of the training. If we could take any necessary actions to "move" more people from the left portions of this distribution to the far right portion, then we would be increasing ROI and impact. This is exactly the principal aim of the SCM—to "grow" ROI and increasingly leverage more results from training.

We know from the interview phase of the study both the value of success and the factors that enable success. This allows us to make a business case for growing the far right side of the distribution in the illustration. We can ask, for instance, what the value would be if we could grow the number of successful application instances by 10 percent. Then, we can ask what it might take to attempt this, such as getting more managers to support the training, or getting more trainees to use the same job aid their successful counterparts used.

We should also point out that it is not always necessary to make conclusions about impact in terms of dollar values. We used such values in the preceding example only to make the case simple and clear. In SCM practice, we encounter many instances in which programs that do not entail such simply translated results can likewise benefit greatly from SCM methods.

Summary

This, in a nutshell, is how the SCM works. First, a survey (or sometimes another information-harvesting method) is used to gauge the overall distribution of reported success and nonsuccess. This is followed by an in-depth interview phase in which we sample cases from each extreme of the distribution and dig deep to understand, analyze, and document, in clear and inarguable terms, the specific nature of exactly how the training was used (if it was) and exactly what verifiable results it led to (if any). The standard of evidence is the same as we would use in a court of law; it must be provable beyond a reasonable doubt, documentable, verifiable, and compelling.

From this investigation, we are able to answer the following questions:

- When training works, what value does it help achieve?
- How frequently and at what rate does it work this well?
- When it works, why? What factors help or hinder results?
- What is the value lost when training does not work?
- What is the case for making it work better?
- What would it take to make it work better? Would such efforts be worthwhile?

CHAPTER 14

So What? Now What?

Andrew Jefferson and Roy Pollock

In this chapter, two training experts provide their recommendations on how to approach program evaluation from the perspective of the business to ensure that its needs—as the "customer" of training programs—are met.

The Questions That Need to Be Answered

As business managers, we have reviewed hundreds of presentations and reports. The questions we wanted answered were always the same: So what? Now what?

In other words, what did we learn from the initiative: *so what?* And, therefore, what should we do in the future: *now what?* It did not matter whether the initiative was a marketing program, an R&D project, or training. It did not matter whether the initiative was a smashing success or an abject failure. What we wanted to know was: what did it teach us about what we should do going forward?

Of course, everyone is happy when an initiative has been a success—that is, when it has achieved the goals for which it was created. Even so, a manager who reports such a success must also be able to explain the critical success factors or recommend future actions to make similar initiatives even more effective. Arie de Geus (2002) was right: the only way to stay ahead of the competition is to learn faster than they do, and the only way to improve learning effectiveness is to critically evaluate what you have done.

Enlightened organizations are willing to accept the occasional failure, so long as something was learned in the process. Indeed, as Peters and Waterman (1982) pointed out years ago in *In Search of Excellence*, "If you are not having some failures, you are not trying hard enough." The most important responsibility of business

managers is to deploy the company's resources—time, money, and talent—to maximize the probability of sustainable success. To do so, managers need relevant, reliable, and compelling program evaluations to make informed decisions.

So, for a business manager, evaluation is never optional; it is the lifeblood of the
organization and essential to its survival. The need for meaningful evaluation applies
to training programs just as it does to every other business process.

A Business Person's Criteria

The Kirkpatrick Model has stood the test of time as the leading taxonomy of evaluation for trainers, but it is not often executed in the way that business managers
think about program evaluation. Business managers need to know: "Did the program
achieve its objectives?"

When training providers talk about "levels of evaluation" to business managers,
it hurts rather than enhances their credibility as business partners because it sounds
like learning jargon. If you want to be successful in a corporate setting, express your
results in the terms and concepts used by business leaders. As Sullivan (2005) re-
minds us, "History has proven that managers will not learn your language or shift to
your focus, so it is you who must adapt."

Business managers judge evaluations using four criteria: relevant, credible, compelling, and efficient. From a business leader's perspective, an evaluation is successful only if it clears all four hurdles; any one can trip you up (Figure 14.1).

Figure 14-1. Four Hurdles

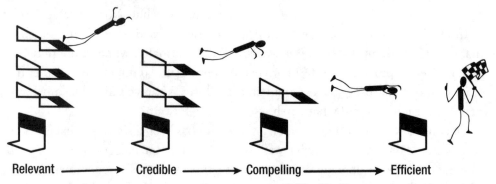

Relevant ⟶ Credible ⟶ Compelling ⟶ Efficient

© *The 6Ds Company, used with permission.*

PDCA Cycle

A fundamental concept of process improvement is the PDCA Cycle (Figure 14-2).
The core concept is that in every cycle, you Plan what you are going to do, you Do

it, you then Check the results and, based on the outcomes, you Act on the findings to adjust the plan for the next cycle.

Figure 14-2. The PDCA Cycle of Continuous Improvement

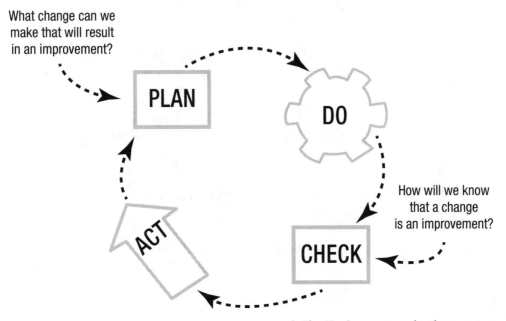

What are we trying to accomplish?

What change can we make that will result in an improvement?

PLAN

DO

ACT

CHECK

How will we know that a change is an improvement?

© The 6Ds Company, used with permission.

The "Check" step, which aligns with the "Monitor and Adjust" box in the New World Kirkpatrick Model, is critical. Unless you meaningfully assess the results, you have no idea whether the process is working, getting better, or getting worse. As Josh Bersin (2008) has noted, "The purpose of measuring any business process is to obtain *actionable information for improvement.*"

When it comes to taking action on a learning initiative, there are only five options: expand it, continue it, revise it, scale it back, or kill it altogether (Figure 14-3).

What Management Wants to Know

At the end of the day, what business managers want to know about a training initiative to make resource-allocation decisions is, "Was it worth it?" That is, did the results justify the time, money, and effort? And, therefore, should the approach be expanded, continued, modified, or abandoned?

It is important to keep in mind that "worth" is subjective. It depends on the business manager and the circumstances. Outcomes that might be deemed worthwhile

Figure 14-3. Management Needs Data

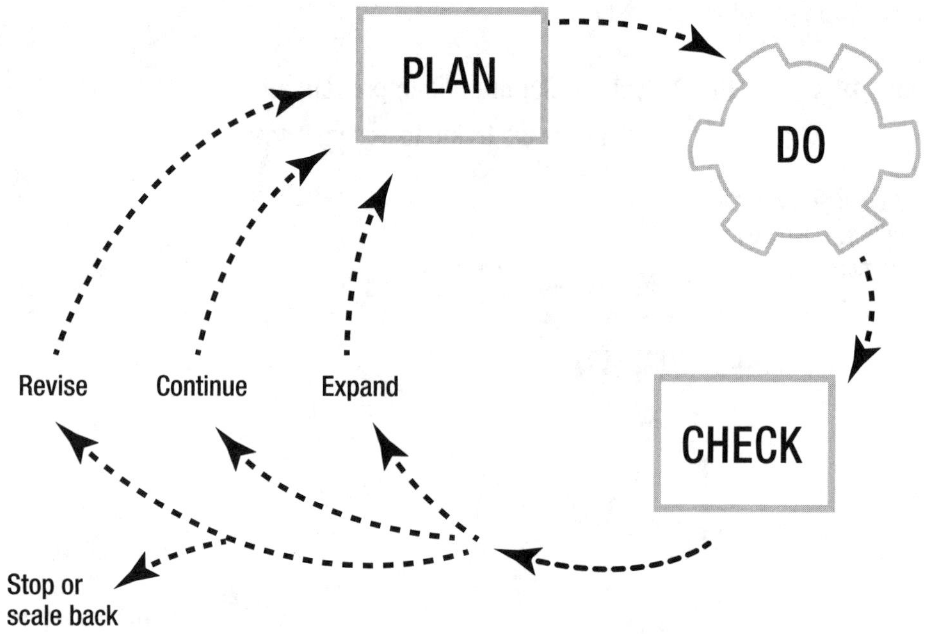

Management needs data to decide which option is the right one for each learning initiative.

© *The 6Ds Company, used with permission.*

in one context or organization might not be considered sufficient in another organization or situation. That is why it is so critical to discuss the business sponsor's definition of success at the very beginning of a training initiative.

It is tragic, wasteful, and potentially career limiting to assume that you know what the sponsor wants and to conduct an evaluation without first checking that the business leaders will find it relevant, credible, and compelling. Some management teams will insist that you try to calculate an ROI, while others will find it unreliable and a waste of time (Pollock, Jefferson, and Wick 2015). There is no single, universal approach or standard that can be applied to all programs.

Outputs Versus Outcomes

A logic model illustrates the "theory of change" behind a training initiative. It sets forth the critical elements and their interrelationships—how each is expected to contribute to the desired outcomes. The approach is widely used in evaluating large-scale change initiatives (Frechtling 2007) and has proven valuable for designing and evaluating corporate learning initiatives (Parskey 2014).

The "theory of change" for company-facilitated learning is shown in the high-level logic map: resources (time and money) are invested in activities (training, coaching, and performance support, for example). The activities generate outputs (number of people trained, number of coaching sessions, number of e-learning modules completed, and so forth), which are expected to lead to outcomes of interest (such as increased sales, faster cycle times, and enhanced employee engagement) (Figure 14-4).

Figure 14-4. A Logic Model Shows Relationships Among Resources, Activities, Outputs, and Outcomes

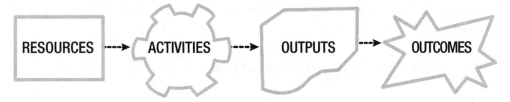

© *The 6Ds Company, used with permission.*

The distinction between outputs and outcomes is important. Outputs are measures of the process activities, such as the number of people trained or the percentage of participants who receive support from their managers. It is important to track outputs to be sure that the program is being executed as planned. For example, it is well known that active support from learners' supervisors is a key element of the learning transfer climate (Holton, Bates, and Ruona 2000). If managerial support is assumed as part of the logic model, then it is important to assess whether or not it is actually occurring. Suboptimal execution of this element of the model will have a detrimental impact on the success of the whole program (that is, whether or not it achieves the desired outcomes).

Outputs themselves, however, do not prove worth. Business managers want to know the outcomes. Reporting how many people you trained or how positively they reacted to the program doesn't mean anything unless you also have outcome measures. Outputs only measure the activity (what it cost the business). They do not assess the value created. Therefore, by themselves, they are insufficient to guide future action.

But what counts as outcomes?

That depends on the nature of the business challenge, the training program, and the proclivities of the business manager or team. The ultimate goal of any training initiative is to positively impact performance to improve business objectives. So, ultimately, the success of a training initiative is determined by the extent to which it improved performance and whether the outcomes achieved were worth the investment. Typical outcomes that business managers value include items such as increased customer satisfaction, reduction in employee turnover, increased sales, higher output, reduced waste or scrap, and generally things that correlate to leading indicators in the New World Kirkpatrick Model.

Proving business results, however, is difficult to do in ways that are credible and compelling because of the myriad other factors that impact a company's or business unit's performance. It is difficult to dissect out, convincingly, the part that training played. It is also usually unnecessary.

Managers request training because they already know that if they can get workers to perform in new and more effective ways (take specific actions or exhibit certain behaviors on the job), then the results will follow (Figure 14-5). It is not necessary for the training department to re-prove the linkage between behavior and results; management already accepts that. What trainers need to show is that the training, plus the on-the-job support from managers (the two are inseparable), has changed behavior in the desired direction.

Figure 14-5. The Fundamental Logic of Training

The fundamental logic of training: Management requests training because they want to improve results; they know that specific actions and behaviors are needed.

© *The 6Ds Company, used with permission.*

Behaviors (Level 3) have to change first for the leading indicators of success to occur. If employees do not change their behaviors following training, then any change in results is due to something other than training. Thus, for many managers, relevant, credible, and compelling evidence of behavior change is sufficient.

Assessing behaviors also has the advantage of yielding results more quickly. In business, time is of the essence. Managers need to know as soon as possible whether an initiative is working or not so that appropriate action can be taken to accelerate it, revise it, or try something else. An evaluation that takes six months to complete is likely to be too late to be useful, no matter how positive the results. Again, this correlates to the "Monitor and Adjust" box in the New World Kirkpatrick Model.

Summary

From a business manager's point of view, evaluation must provide sound evidence for future decision making. It must analyze outcomes of interest (not just the outputs of activity) that are directly related to the business rationale for the program. It must do so in a way that is believable, trustworthy, and sufficiently timely to support relevant action. The findings should be accompanied by clear recommendations based on the data and analysis. When training departments document and report results in this way, they earn a true seat at the management table.

References

Alliger, G., S. Tannenbaum, W. Bennett Jr., H. Traver, and A. Shotland. 1997. "A Meta-Analysis of the Relations Among Training Criteria." *Personnel Psychology*, 50:2, 341–358.

Bersin, J. 2008. *The Training Measurement Book*. San Francisco, CA: Pfeiffer.

de Geus, A. 2002. *The Living Company*. Boston, MA: Harvard Business Review Press.

Donohoe, J., P. Beech, K. Bell-Wright, J. Kirkpatrick, and W. Kirkpatrick. 2014. "How We Used Measurement to Drive 'SOAR—Service Over and Above the Rest.' " In *The Field Guide to the 6Ds: How to Use the Six Disciplines to Transform Learning into Business Results*, 503–512, by R. Pollock, A. Jefferson, and C. Wick. San Francisco, CA: Wiley.

Frechtling, J.A. 2007. *Logic Modeling Methods in Program Evaluation*. San Francisco, CA: Jossey-Bass.

Holton III, E., R. Bates, and W. Ruona. 2000. "Development of a Generalized Learning Transfer System Inventory." *Human Resource Development Quarterly*, 11:4, 333–360.

Parskey, P. 2014. "How We Guide Our Clients to Design with the End in Mind." In *The Field Guide to the 6Ds: How to Use the Six Disciplines to Transform Learning into Business Results*, by R. Pollock, A. Jefferson, and C. Wick, 495–502. San Francisco, CA: Wiley.

Peters, T.J., and R.H. Waterman, Jr. 1982. *In Search of Excellence: Lessons from America's Best-Run Companies*. New York: HarperCollins.

Pollock, R., A. Jefferson, and C. Wick. 2015. *The Six Disciplines of Breakthrough Learning: How to Turn Training and Development into Business Results*. Hoboken, NJ: Wiley.

Sullivan, J. 2005. "Measuring the Impact of Executive Development." In *The Future of Executive Development*, edited by J. Bolt, 260–284. New York: Executive Development Associates.

CHAPTER 15

Reporting Progress and Demonstrating Program Value

It is interesting how many training professionals say that their organizations don't value them, but when questioned about how they share evaluation-related data, they say they do not really have good methods. Providing the data defined during the planning process in a timely and easy-to-understand manner during implementation is a strong step toward becoming a learning and performance consultant.

While the focus of this book is on how to evaluate programs, the desired outcome is typically to be able to demonstrate the value the program has brought to the organization. This chapter provides guidance for reporting interim program progress to participants, managers, and stakeholders and for delivering a final report of program outcomes.

Sharing Training Outcomes

Immediately after training, report on training outcomes and initiate the on-the-job performance support package. Remember that line managers and stakeholders are usually not interested in a lot of detail about the training program, but sharing a few, key items can be helpful.

For example, if testing was included in the training, you could share the test scores and comment on the overall knowledge level of participants. This is the time to share any concerns about confidence and commitment to perform the new skills on the job and discuss how to remedy them. If the training outcome was positive, it never hurts to share a few favorable comments from evaluation forms or transcriptions of verbal feedback.

This is a place to show your value as a learning and performance consultant—helping managers to start implementation on the right foot and offering your support.

Reporting Program Progress

During implementation, set automatic calendar reminders and tasks for yourself to check on and report progress both formally and informally.

Hold regular meetings, or "touchpoints," that were agreed to and scheduled during the planning phase with managers and perhaps key stakeholders. These are opportunities for each group to report their own observations and findings, and to discuss what is and is not working, with the goal of keeping the initiative on track.

When people know they will be asked to report their progress, they do not want to show up with nothing to share. The mere existence of the touchpoint actually drives the performance and outcomes and creates the data for you to report.

Touchpoints are also an opportunity to showcase the Bright Lights™. These stories show the most positive performance and results as a good example, as well as a demonstration of the initiative's value.

These regular meetings may serve as your interim "reporting" vehicle, depending upon who is present. Or, they may be a good place to gather data that you repackage to communicate to the organization in some other fashion.

As the initiative goes on, continue to validate your value as a learning and performance consultant by insisting on regular touchpoints, sharing results, and moderating the resolution of barriers. This helpful, strategic interaction with the business in an ongoing fashion solidifies your role as a business partner.

Using Dashboards to Report Program Progress

A simple and effective way to share key program data and to visualize program progress toward the defined goals is with a dashboard. Like the regular touchpoints, the dashboard not only shows current program status but can also drive performance and results with its mere existence. No one wants to have a substandard number displayed for the whole organization to see.

Dashboards are dynamic, and they invite cross-functional review and subsequent decision making. Areas below standard are clearly displayed so that those involved in the initiative can discuss them and determine what plan modifications or intervention may be required to get them back on track.

Many find it helpful to consider a dashboard in a car when explaining the purpose of a dashboard for an initiative. The primary time to make good use of a dashboard in a car is when the car is moving. Information about speed, oil pressure, fuel level, and system status alert the driver to potential problems before they negatively affect the car or the driver, such as in the case of a potential breakdown, speeding ticket, empty gas tank, or the like. Using a dashboard after arriving in your garage is of little value other than being able to see how far you drove.

The same is true for learning and performance dashboards. They are most useful when used during program execution to drive, track, and report program status.

When things are going well, the dashboard is a great encourager, and sometimes even a reward. When things are not going as well, the dashboard is a catalyst to identify and fix problems before the progress of the initiative and ultimate goal accomplishment are compromised.

Your dashboard should contain critical behavior and required driver performance levels, as well as leading-indicator status. You may want to include one key item from learning, such as confidence to apply, or percentage of employees who have completed training for longer initiatives. The bulk of the dashboard, however, should focus on Levels 3 and 4.

Electronic Medical Record (EMR) Implementation Program Dashboard Example

Electronic medical record (EMR) systems, when used consistently by nurses and others who chart patient data, ultimately improve patient care and safety outcomes by reducing medication errors. They also reduce the related costs of additional care required to remedy errors, and any lawsuits that may ensue. The importance of EMR compliance from both a patient care and financial standpoint makes system implementation and usage mission critical.

This dashboard example is a modified representation of a real dashboard used by a healthcare organization during their EMR implementation (Table 15-1). The actual data have been changed because of sensitivity.

The items included in the dashboard were selected as key areas to drive, track, and report for the success of the initiative. The items above the bold line are selected required drivers and the critical behavior.

Charting records in the EMR is the critical behavior for nurses and other healthcare professionals. They are required to enter 100 percent of patient records into the new EMR system instead of using the former paper forms.

Auditing charts for compliance is a required driver. Supervisors have been tasked with checking patient charts at the end of each shift to ensure that all records were entered at least to the minimum standards.

Quality control audits both the presence and quality of the electronic records for each patient, as well as supervisors' access and review of each chart at the end of the shift. These data are reported to populate the dashboard.

Discussing charting during staff meetings is a required driver. Because this initiative is mission critical, unit leaders have been asked to include EMR charting as an agenda item during every meeting. After each meeting, meeting notes are audited to ensure that the topic was discussed.

Four leading indicators are reported below the bold line. Reduction of medication errors is the earliest outcome that results from charting to standard. It is easily tracked by counting incident reports. With reduced medication errors, the related

Table 15-1. EMR Implementation Progress

Report date: April 2016 (Four months after training)

ACTION/RESULT	TARGET	ACTUAL	PREVIOUS MONTH	RATING
Records charted to standard in EMR	100%	86%	85%	😐
Charts audited for compliance	90%	91%	88%	🙂
Charting discussed during staff meetings	100%	70%	75%	🙁
Reduction of medication errors	40%	29%	30%	😐
Medication error-related adverse events	0.5%	1.3%	1.5%	🙁
Medication error-related medical costs	$30,000	$79,000	$78,000	🙁
Increase in patient satisfaction	10%	8%	3%	🙂
Medication error-related legal claims	4	5	6	😐

adverse effects, additional medical costs, and legal claims should also eventually decrease. During all of this, patient satisfaction should increase, which is a major factor in the amounts of insurance reimbursements.

The dashboard is updated monthly. The "Target" is the goal set for each month, the "Actual" column reports the most recent data, and "Previous Month" is provided as a comparison. The "Rating" is a subjective judgment of the current status or progress for each item.

In the current month, the EMR initiative is not doing terribly well. While charting has improved slightly, the rate is still significantly below the target of 100 percent. Not surprisingly, the importance of charting has clearly not been punctuated during every staff meeting as required. Since an acceptable level of charting has not been occurring, all of the outcomes remain lower than target. The situation is not likely to improve until all required drivers are properly engaged.

Making an Impactful Final Report

Do not be intimidated by the idea of reporting final program results. In this case, less is more. It is not effective to create lengthy written reports. Not only will a long report typically not be read, but you also introduce so many opportunities for questions on esoteric items outside of the final goal of showing that the training has increased performance and positively affected targeted organizational results.

It may also be assuring to know that most stakeholders are more satisfied with evidence than they are seeking for you to prove something. For example, a senior learning manager in an intelligence agency reports that her stakeholders understand that there is more than one contributor to any outcome. So, she focuses on providing numerous pieces of evidence related to how training helped the staff to do their jobs better, and then she connects evidence to their testimonials and data on key outcomes. This chain of evidence is effective in showing the value of training for performance and ultimate results.

Strive to create a brief, graphical presentation that you deliver to stakeholders in person whenever possible. Start by reminding them of the program purpose and the problem you were trying to solve. Recap the program methodology. Then, share your Levels 3 and 4 findings in plain language. Highlight the success factors that most contributed to the outcomes, noting that these celebrate the teamwork of training, managers, support departments, stakeholders, and the training participants themselves. The training itself is often a noted success factor, so this creates a natural opportunity to briefly highlight key training data related to knowledge, skill, attitude, confidence, and commitment.

Then, have the courage to share the barriers that were encountered along the way, as well as how they were resolved, or how they could be resolved in future initiatives. Close with recommendations for improving future results and other mission-critical initiatives. Deliver a report with this data, and you will earn learning and performance consultant status.

A good report includes a balance of qualitative and quantitative data. A report including only numeric data is a snooze; no one wants to read it, no matter how impressive the numbers. However, a report that contains only testimonials, stories, and anecdotes does not have enough credibility. The power is in providing numeric data that is illustrated or supported by a testimonial or story from someone involved in the initiative.

For example, part of the final report presentation for a leadership development program could be:

One of the key deliverables after the offsite leadership development program was for leaders to work with their direct reports to customize career plans and specific steps to make those plans a reality. Currently, 92 percent of direct reports have defined career plans.

In the annual employee survey, the employee engagement score has increased 12 percent over the prior year, and turnover has decreased 10 percent. One young woman, in particular, was so affected by the new guidance provided by her supervisor that she stopped in to the training office to thank us. But instead of us telling her story, we would like to have her tell you herself. Erin?

Hello, my name is Erin Williams. I started here at Optima Systems about two years ago. Honestly, over the holidays last year, I was on the Internet searching for my next opportunity. I didn't really have a specific reason; I just didn't really feel connected here. After the holidays, my supervisor, Susan Gomez, set up a meeting with me to talk about my career here. We talked about my degree, my interests, and where I saw myself going in the company.

We put together a plan, including some training, and also dedicated time together to help me to earn a promotion to senior analyst within the next two years. I'm excited to say that I have been doing the training, and Susan says I am on track to be able to apply for one of the positions soon.

I am so thankful to all of you, to Susan, and to Optima Systems for believing in me and helping me to reach my goals. I can't imagine working anywhere else.

Every written report is unique and should be adapted to meet stakeholder requests. Since we are often asked for templates and examples, there are actual final reports included in Part 4 of this book. They are not templates and should not be copied and followed; rather, they are examples to show the variety of formats that final reports might take based on differing program and organizational needs.

Summary

Demonstrating the value a training program has brought to an organization is a key step in graduating from being a trainer to a learning and performance consultant.

Immediately after training, briefly report on key training outcomes and initiate the on-the-job performance support package. During implementation, regularly check on and report progress both formally and informally. Insist on these regular touch points to keep the initiative going, and to solidify your value as a learning and performance consultant. A dashboard can be an effective way to report interim program progress in an easy-to-understand format.

Many training professionals are intimidated by the idea of creating a final program report. Focus on making the report brief and graphical. Include a blend of quantitative and qualitative data to create credibility and interest. Use what you know about your stakeholder priorities and preferences to make a report that appeals to and is meaningful to them. When possible, bring a graduate with you to share a personal success story.

CHAPTER 16

Avoiding Common Evaluation Pitfalls

Throughout this book, we've stressed that the four levels have not necessarily been implemented correctly over the past decades. On the contrary, misconceptions and misapplication have reduced their simple effectiveness. This book is an attempt to correct common misinformation and misapplication so that your implementation is as successful as possible. This chapter serves as a final reminder of the most common pitfalls and how to avoid them in your work.

Pitfall #1: Addressing Evaluation Requirements After a Program Has Launched

Many training professionals mistakenly design, develop, and deliver a training program, and only then start to think about how they will evaluate its effectiveness. The traditional ADDIE (analyze, design, develop, implement, evaluate) model of instructional design reinforces this damaging belief. Using this approach nearly guarantees that there will be little or no value to report.

We received a phone call from a consultant a few years back. He was quite proud to tell us about the multimillion-dollar leadership development program he had created for a large corporation. He worked with them to define their needs before developing the three-year program, which was nearing the end of the first year. He was contacting us to find out if we wished to join the project as evaluation consultants, as they had data from the first year of program participation.

When we get calls like that one, our hearts sink. We asked just a few questions to verify our suspicion: they had not pinpointed the specific leading indicators they hoped this large investment would positively affect. Of even more concern, they had not identified critical behaviors for the managers involved in the program, nor had they prepped senior managers to coach and monitor performance. Ultimately, they had created a "nice to have" program containing a laundry list of development activities targeted to nothing in particular.

We had no choice but to tell this well-meaning consultant that there was little we could do to help them, other than recommend that as quickly as possible he enroll in one of our training programs to learn how to create an effective program plan for the next time, and see if there is anything they can salvage from the current misguided program.

To avoid this pitfall, programs should begin with a focus on the Level 4 Results you need to accomplish. This automatically focuses efforts on what is most important. Conversely, if you follow the common, old-school approach to planning and implementing your training, thinking about how you will evaluate Level 1 Reaction, then Level 2 Learning, then Level 3 Behavior, it's easy to see why few people get to Level 4 Results in this fashion.

Set yourself apart from and ahead of the crowd by using the four levels upside down; start every project by first considering the leading indicators you plan to influence and articulate how this will contribute to the Level 4 Result of your organization. Then, think about what really needs to occur on the job to produce good results (Level 3). Consider next what training or other support is required for workers to perform well on the job (Level 2). Finally, consider what type of training will be conducive to imparting the required skills successfully (Level 1).

Pitfall #2: Viewing All Training Programs as Equal

You may be thinking that the resources required to evaluate all of your training programs at all four levels are simply not available. Set your worries aside; this is not the recommendation. All programs are not created equal, and only those that are the most mission critical for an organization should have an entire four levels evaluation plan created and implemented for them. From there, the less impact a program has on the bottom line or mission accomplishment, the less that should be invested in evaluation at any level.

During the program planning phase, think about each program through the lens of the four levels, starting with Level 4. If you are not able to easily articulate how the program contributes organizationally, then it is probably not a good candidate for a robust evaluation plan. It would not be a good use of resources. However, taking this moment to consider the Level 4 impact of every program is a good practice to prioritize the relative importance of each program.

Pitfall #3: Spending the Majority of Your Training Evaluation Resources on Levels 1 and 2

Similar to how not every training program has equal importance to an organization, the four levels themselves are also not equal in importance. Generally speaking, Level 3 is the most important level to not only evaluate but also to invest in for any important program. Without on-the-job application, training has no hope of contributing to organizational results, and therefore is of little value to the organization. If your program is important enough to have a Level 3 plan, then it is also important enough to have leading indicators established, as well as evaluation of Level 4 Results.

The evaluation of Level 2 is important to ensure that training participants leave training prepared with the required knowledge and skill. However, proper Level 2 evaluation can be built right into the design of a program and should therefore not become an evaluation resource priority.

Level 1 is the least important level. Of course you want to know that the training was well received, but consider how much of a resource investment it is worth to gather this data. The investment should be quite small. Focus on formative methods, and only formally evaluate the few key items you plan to analyze and actually use.

Consider the relative importance of the levels in light of industry data. The 2016 ATD report *Evaluating Learning: Getting to Measurements That Matter* polled 199 learning professionals, more than 80 percent of whom hold the title of manager, director, or executive, revealing that they are investing nearly 70 percent of their training evaluation resources in Levels 1 and 2. Sadly, this statistic did not improve since ATD's previous report in 2009. This old-school approach of spending heavily on effective training leaves few resources for the more important job of ensuring training effectiveness at Levels 3 and 4.

To have sufficient resources to implement a quality Level 3 plan, streamline evaluation at Levels 1 and 2. Carefully consider what information is useful to the training department to ensure that training is of sufficient quality, as well as what information is required by stakeholders, if any, at these levels. If you do not have an intentional plan to use a particular piece of data, save resources by choosing not to gather it.

Now that you've saved resources for Levels 3 and 4, what level of effort and resource investment can you expect to devote to each? Level 4 Results is actually the simplest and least resource intensive to evaluate. If something is a true Level 4 result, it is important enough that someone in the organization is already measuring and monitoring it, and it is simply a matter of obtaining the data. What is more difficult is to find the connection between training, on-the-job performance, and organizational results. In many evaluation plans, the missing link is Level 3.

A strong Level 3 plan recommended for important initiatives will be resource intensive. This is the level to which most of the resources you saved by streamlining your Levels 1 and 2 efforts will transfer; however, evaluating Level 3 is not as expensive as some would think. When tools and systems are constructed at the same time as the program itself, and ultimately viewed as part of the program, this simply reallocates the resources from instructional design to performance support.

Pitfall #4: Relying Solely on Standardized Surveys

Some trainers believe in the existence of a miracle survey that will give them all of the training evaluation data they need. Don't buy it. For mission-critical programs, it is important to employ multiple evaluation methods and tools to create a credible chain of evidence showing that training improved job performance and contributed measurably to organizational results. For less important programs, you will want to be equally careful about selecting the few evaluation items you require.

Surveys, particularly those administered and tabulated electronically, are a wonderfully efficient means of gathering data. However, response rates tend to be low, and there is a limit to the types of information that can be gathered. It is so easy to disseminate these surveys that they are often launched after every program, no matter how large or small. The questions are not customized to the program or the need for data, and participants can become wary of such a survey cycle. This creates survey fatigue and makes it less likely that you will gather meaningful data for any program.

For mission-critical programs in particular, gather both quantitative (numeric) and qualitative (descriptive) data. Open-ended survey questions can gather quantitative data to some degree, but adding another evaluation method provides better data. For example, a post-program survey could be administered, and results analyzed. If a particular trend is identified, a sampling of program participants could be interviewed and asked open-ended questions on a key topic.

When people think of interviews, the words *time consuming* and *expensive* often come to mind. Depending upon the rigor required by your stakeholders, you may be able to obtain good interview data by simply calling or briefly visiting training participants and asking them a question. Don't be too intimidated to integrate this human element into your program evaluation data.

An often overlooked source of evaluation data is formative data. Build formal time into your training programs for facilitators to solicit participant feedback, and ask your facilitators for their feedback via a survey or interview after the program.

Pitfall #5: Asking Questions That Don't Generate Useful Data

The overuse of standardized surveys in pitfall #4 can be one contributor to pitfall #5: evaluation questions that do not generate useful data. The first cause of this is including questions that are not terribly important for a given program, as is common with overly standardized surveys. If you do not have a ready use for the data, the question should not be asked. It's a waste of resources all around. If you don't need the information, then it is likely that the person completing the survey is going to have a similar level of disinterest in answering the question.

Another reason that some questions don't generate useful data is the way they are phrased. For further discussion on this topic, refer to chapter 10, which covers the importance of phrasing questions neutrally, and chapter 11, which describes how to construct questions from the perspective of the learner.

If you are not getting an acceptable response rate to your surveys, if you sense that people are simply completing them as quickly as possible, or you get few, if any, comments, the problem might be the questions you ask, and how you go about asking them.

Pitfall #6: Making Evaluation Too Complicated or Academic

While the more common pitfall is to attempt to overly automate and simplify training evaluation to the point that it is nearly useless, there is a smaller camp of training professionals that go in the polar opposite direction by making evaluation so academic and complicated that only a statistician could understand it.

These individuals are typically found in academic institutions and government and military organizations that have a higher level of rigor and greater need for valid and reliable data than the private sector. With that said, these individuals are attempting to create something that is just too big and scientific to work even within their own organizations.

If your presentations of training data generally involve charts that require a magnifying glass to decipher, or your reports exceed 25 pages in length, you are experiencing this pitfall. Connect with your stakeholders to find out what is most important to them and refocus your efforts on gathering data to support their needs. Do all you can to remove jargon and complication. Be more like Apple than Microsoft. Try out your new approach on a few people outside of the training industry entirely. If they can understand your message, you are on the right track.

Pitfall #7: Not Using Collected Data

Have you ever inherited an office that had a precariously tall stack of papers in one corner, next to a stuffed file cabinet? Wendy did, and upon closer inspection, she saw that it was years and years of old training evaluation forms.

Besides a poor document retention system, the bigger problem this indicated was that the evaluations had not been properly analyzed, and findings were not appropriately integrated into program enhancements and performance-support efforts. When Wendy asked around the department, multiple individuals commented that there was never time or resources to tabulate the evaluations, so a quick flip through them by the facilitator or the manager was all that ever really happened. "Someday" someone would enter the data into some type of system so that it could be quantified and analyzed. But "someday" had not occurred for years.

When you survey a group of individuals, you are making an implicit agreement with them that you will act upon their aggregated feedback. Continuing to disseminate surveys when the participants can clearly see that you are doing nothing with the data will quickly create the expectation that nothing ever will happen with their feedback, and they will stop giving it.

At that same organization, Wendy was asked to create an evaluation form to use after a week-long event in which new products and updates were launched to the sales and customer service team. She included questions about the program quality and content, the meeting facilities, and how the participants felt about selling the new products.

Wendy was present when the vice president of marketing, who organized the event, first reviewed the evaluations. His commentary went something like this:

Joe said that the new product will not sell in his market because the color scheme doesn't work with Midwestern homes. Maybe that's why his sales are so low.

Sue complained about the food. We can't make everyone happy.

A few people said it was too cold . . . there's nothing we can do about the temperature of a hotel ballroom.

You get the point. He had a reason to dismiss every comment. Future meetings didn't change, nor did the questions on the evaluation form. No response to legitimate product concerns, such as inappropriateness of a product for a given market, was issued. The result? Each event received less and less feedback, or the infamous line down the side of the page to select "all fives." The marketing vice president was satisfied with this; he assumed that meant that everyone was happy, or at least they were off his back.

We sincerely hope that you are more interested in learning from your program participants, and that you want to continually improve your programs to assist them in successfully performing in their jobs. Make sure you can and do review any evaluation data you receive and make a point to show how it's being used.

After each of the five sessions of our online certification program, we gather data. At the beginning of each session, the feedback from the previous session, as well as any related questions, are debriefed. Participants often comment that they are so pleased to be heard and proud when they see us implement one of their suggestions. This feedback also provides an opportunity to fully explain when we are unable to implement certain suggestions, so participants know they were considered.

Summary

Misconceptions and misapplication of the four levels over the past decades have reduced their simple effectiveness. These common occurrences can be corrected to maximize program value.

Build your evaluation plan during the instructional design process and implement it throughout program execution. If you wait until the program is created, and worse, until it has been delivered, it is way too late to create an evaluation plan that will yield useful data, and a program that will ultimately deliver the intended results.

Consider the organizational importance of the program when designing the evaluation plan and tools, and use this as a guide for the amount of resources it warrants. Customize evaluation methods and tools so that items yield useful data that will actually be used to maximize program outcomes. Focus on Level 3, the most important level, when considering where to spend your valuable resources.

Resist the temptation of a "one-size-fits-all" standardized survey, which will only waste resources and frustrate those who have to complete it. By the same token, don't create such a complicated, detailed plan that only a statistician can implement it and interpret the findings.

Use a common-sense, integrated approach to training evaluation, and the resources you invest in it will yield meaningful data that you can use to maximize and demonstrate program value.

References

ASTD Research. 2009. *The Value of Evaluation: Making Training Evaluations More Effective*. Alexandria, VA: ASTD Press.

ATD Research. 2016. *Evaluating Learning: Getting to Measurements That Matter*. Alexandria, VA: ATD Press.

PART 4

Case Studies

One of the most common requests we receive is for case examples. On the surface, this seems perfectly reasonable. Training professionals would like to learn from their peers and see how they have gone about applying these principles so they can do something similar. Our concern is that case examples are not viewed as examples but rather as templates or the formula to follow for every similar type of program. We are reminded of this underlying concern nearly daily, as trainers write to us and say, "Could you please give me an example of a large U.S.-based manufacturing company that is starting a leadership development program?" Or, "Our organization is not-for-profit, so this example from a corporation doesn't fit for us." In our opinion, the nature of the program in question is such that it does fit well enough for training professionals to glean a few ideas and some structural guidance to create their own programs that meets their unique needs.

We say all this as a caution that these examples are just that: examples. They are not fill-in-the-blank forms that will work for you, your program, or your organization. Learn from what each example shares in terms of how they went about determining the program needs, meeting them, and then documenting their success. Examine how they adjusted their plans during implementation and stayed on track to the maximum level of results. Put all of this through the filter of what works in your organization, with your culture and available resources. Just because it worked for them does not ensure that it will work for you.

With that said, enjoy these case examples that show that regular people can and do implement these principles successfully in their work every day. Keep in mind that the New World Model is about developing a compelling chain of evidence consisting of the proper blend of quantitative and qualitative data. It is about providing the stakeholders with a preponderance of evidence, not proof.

CHAPTER 17

Common Practice in Leadership Program: Greencore Northampton

Paul Aggett

Greencore Group, a leading international manufacturer of convenience foods, supplies a wide range of chilled, frozen, and ambient foods to retail and food-service customers in the United States and the United Kingdom. The business is currently experiencing exponential growth and in need of leaders who can adapt to this dynamic environment and meet both the needs of employees and the demands of the business environment.

The Common Practice in Leadership Program was established to support the functional heads of Greencore Group and to assist them in developing both as individuals and as team leaders capable of leading the business into the future. Greencore Northampton, located 70 miles north of London, United Kingdom, was chosen as the site for the pilot program.

Stakeholder Expectations

Stakeholder expectations, in the likely order in which they would occur, were as follows:

- improved capability of the senior managers
- increase in planning for longer term
- organizational fit and readiness for next growth phase
- improved teamwork within and between functional areas
- improved performance of employees under the new leadership
- reduced costs
- increased sales
- increased profits.

Program Structure

The pilot for this program ran with six carefully chosen managers from different functions who did not usually work closely together. Jamie Richardson of the Whittlebury Academy, a U.K.-based training and conference center, and I developed the program and its evaluation methodologies. The program ran over four months, with many additional sessions planned and run by the delegates outside of the scheduled program timings using these modules:

- **Team analysis:** Strength Deployment Inventory (SDI) to enable each person to understand themselves better and also to see themselves in relation to the other members of the program
- **Common practice:** Activities and experiences designed to develop team processes that enable strategic thinking, cross-functional problem solving, 360 communication, and the opportunity to balance decision making with the associated risks and benefits
- **Action learning set and review:** Project review session that allows participants to challenge and learn from each other and provide opportunities to apply the process in the actual work environment
- **Board presentations:** Presentation to the executive team on what was learned during the program, both in terms of personal development and effects on the business and the business challenge results.

Targeted Objectives

Six targeted objectives were created by program developers based on business and employee needs as well as stakeholder expectations.

1. Understand others, which first requires an understanding of self.
2. Realize how motivational differences enhance a team.
3. Develop a common language, which requires a blend of team processes and relationship skills to be added to the already present professional and technical skill sets.
4. Understand the task and the purpose, which will ensure true understanding and consistent quality results.
5. Check or challenge a purpose to build relationships and produce results fit for the purpose of all stakeholders.
6. Understand the difficulty and risk associated with true delegation, but also realize the potential benefits to all concerned when undertaken correctly.

Level 4: Results

The desired outcome defined for this program is to "help drive continued growth, success, and prosperity." This was to be measured by a contribution of increasing revenue through business efficiency and growth.

Internal Leading Indicators

- improved functional alignment toward site's goals
- increased individual and team productivity
- increased engagement score in cultural survey relating to coaching and feedback
- sustained improvement in cross-functional teamwork in business-critical areas
- more internal promotions
- increased employee stability rates
- reduction in recruitment fees for key senior roles
- enhanced culture (from survey and observations)
- improved cost figures
- sustained cost figures
- increased top-line performance.

External Leading Indicators

- increased customer satisfaction
- repeat sales
- new customers
- increased sales.

Level 3: Behavior

Learning objectives were transformed into the following critical behaviors of leaders who were required to create the targeted results:

- Communicate a shared vision with direct reports.
- Consistently use common language.
- Engage in activities to increase relevant self-awareness, such as coaching and checking for common purpose.
- Consistently use defined productive delegation behaviors, including the "Purpose Grid," coaching, feedback, and questioning.
- Check and challenge processes to ensure maximum performance.

Critical behaviors do not happen just because of formal training. The following performance support and accountability methods were developed and implemented to increase the frequency of the behaviors:

- performance job aids
- performance observation and feedback
- interviews and focus groups with leaders and their managers
- mentoring
- one-on-one coaching from supervisors
- formal and informal recognition
- targeted on-the-job training.

Evaluation Methods and Tools

Prior to the program, participants and their managers were sent a development application program request form (Table 17-1). This form was designed to involve participants even before the program began and to set the expectation that they and their managers were to commit to working together after the program to ensure application.

Various forms of in-program checks (formative evaluation) were conducted to ensure a positive reaction and learning. A formal, immediate post-program evaluation was administered as well (Table 17-2).

A training program evaluation form was administered to the directors who manage the training graduates three months after the program was completed to validate that the critical behaviors actually occurred and sustainable change could be seen and measured (Table 17-3).

To gather final feedback from the training graduates, their comments were captured in a questionnaire:

Dear Team,

I am in the process of developing a case study for the recent "Common Practice in Leadership" course we all attended, and I would like your support and help!

Can you please answer the following questions, with as much detail as you can, and return to me at your earliest convenience?

The case study will help me promote the program within Greencore and will also help us promote the program to other organizations.

Thank you in advance.

- Why did I attend the program?
- What did I learn from the program?
- What did I learn about myself?
- What am I doing differently since the program?
- What have I achieved since completing the program?
- What business results have been driven from changes I have made?
- Why would I recommend the program?

Table 17-1. Development Application Course Booking Form

Applicant's Name	
Course Applied For	NLP Diploma in Coaching Practice
Date(s) of Course (if known)	Thursday, November 12; Friday, November 13; and Wednesday, December 9
Line Manager	

Program Aims & Objectives

At the end of the course you will:

- Be aware of your own and others' use of both enabling and inhibiting language patterns, and challenge, with elegance, those patterns to increase awareness and change.
- Communicate in ways that enhance understanding, trust, and interest.
- Recognize the impact of your own and others' nonverbal communication.
- Consider and adopt beliefs of excellence that support your personal and professional goals.
- Motivate yourself and others by determining the values and criteria by which you and others make decisions.
- Set compelling goals for yourself and for others, thus ensuring you and they achieve the results you really want for yourself and the business.
- Coach yourself and others toward achieving both your own and their potential.

Applicant's Learning Objectives

Line Manager's Reasons for Supporting Applicant

Table 17-1. Development Application Course Booking Form *(continued)*

Applicant and Line Manager to read and sign contract on reverse.
No program place is guaranteed until adjoining instructions have been received.

LEARNER'S CONTRACT

I agree that:

- It is my responsibility to complete the development program named above and attend all sessions.
- It is my responsibility, where required, to request support of the development program named above.
- It is my responsibility to have learning outcomes verified as I work through the learning unit, rather than leave it until I have finished.
- It is my responsibility to apply the skills and behaviors that I learn and to seek support and coaching as required.
- I also agree that failure to complete all aspects of this program will result in course costs being charged to my department.

MANAGER'S CONTRACT

I agree that:

- It is my responsibility to ensure that my team member clearly understands the Learning Objectives and expected outcomes associated with this program.
- It is my responsibility to ensure that my team member has adequate time to complete his development.
- It is my responsibility to motivate and support my team member to complete her development. I will coach or provide her additional resources as required.
- It is my responsibility to ensure that my team member applies the knowledge and behaviors he has gained, to ensure that the learning is embedded.
- I also agree that failure to ensure my team member completes all aspects of this program will result in course costs being charged to my department.

Learner's Name	Learner's Signature	Date
Line Manager's Signature	Line Manager's Signature	Date

Table 17-2. Participant Post-Program Evaluation Form

	Training Course Evaluation Form	Form	LD004
		Revision	1
		Revision Date	14/11/2014

Please complete this form to let us know your reaction to this course. Your input will help us to evaluate our efforts, and your comments and suggestions will help us to plan and improve future courses.

Your Name:	Date of Course:
Course Title:	Venue:
Trainer(s):	

Please work through the form and check the relevant box. There is space for free text on the reverse of this form.

Post-Course Reaction		Strongly Disagree	Disagree	Neutral	Agree	Strongly Agree
		-4	-2	0	+2	+4
Me						
1	I was personally interested / motivated in taking this course.					
2	I had the necessary prerequisite knowledge for completing this course.					
3	My manager discussed my attendance in this course with me prior to the event.					
Materials / Environment						
4	The course materials (hand-outs, workbooks, etc.) were relevant / up to date.					
5	The layout / style of the course material helped my learning experience.					
6	There was a good mix of materials (e.g., presentation, video, discussion, exercises, role play).					
7	The group size was right for this course.					
8	Facilities and / or technological equipment were appropriate for the course.					
Relevance						
9	The course content matched the objectives outlined in the instructions.					
10	The course is relevant to the role I perform / my responsibilities.					
11	The course allowed me to relate my existing knowledge and relate it to the new knowledge.					
Effectiveness						
12	I had opportunity to practice, apply, and gain feedback of my learning during the course.					
13	I had opportunity to question and discuss the subject matter during the course.					
14	I will be able to apply this learning to my role.					
15	The tutor(s) were effective, had knowledge of the subject matter, responded fully, and had relevant examples.					
16	Please indicate the overall effectiveness of this course.					

Before the Course					Post-Course Learning Review	After the Course				
-4	-2	0	+2	+4		-4	-2	0	+2	+4
					Ability to clearly plan and articulate the "Purpose" of an activity or project					
					Understanding of the difficultly and risk associated with true delegation and being able to explain the benefits to all concerned when it is undertaken correctly.					
					Ability to describe your MSV and understand other people's MSV					
					Practical understanding of how motivational differences can enhance a team if first they are recognized and accepted					
					Ability to transfer leadership facilitation skills into strategic business goals					

Table 17-2. Participant Post-Program Evaluation Form *(continued)*

	Training Course Evaluation Form	Form	LD004
		Revision	1
		Revision Date	14/11/2014

What did you find most beneficial about the course?

How would you improve the course?

Briefly describe how you will take personal responsibility for using the skills/knowledge you have gained in this program. What support will you require to implement your new skills?

© *Greencore Group plc*

Finally, interviews were conducted with training graduates and their directors to obtain testimonies of success.

Results of Pilot

There were several positive results focusing on both business and individual professional levels:

- The business challenge was delivered in full. Several changes within the business resulted in a weekly reduction of materials usage by, on average, over $30,000. These changes have endured, and there is a 12-week trend indicating that they have resolved the issue.
- Individuals understood more deeply their own motivational values. This enabled them to play to their strengths and moderate their overused traits.
- Colleague engagement was improved, as the ability to listen without solving was enhanced. Team members' ideas were accepted and acted upon.
- Meetings became more effective, purposeful, and shorter; some were deemed irrelevant and cancelled altogether.

Table 17-3. Direct Manager and Learning and Development Officer Delayed Evaluation Form

This section will be completed by your Direct Manager and the Learning and Development Officer after you have returned to your normal role to assess the effectiveness of the course in the workplace.

Review Date:		Direct Manager:	

Direct Managerial – Post-Course Effectiveness Review (to be conducted at least two weeks post course)	After the Course				
	-4	-2	0	+2	+4
The outcomes of the course match the course objectives I discussed with my employee prior to the course.					
The employee demonstrates a full understanding/comprehension of the course subject.					
The employee is applying the skills learned during the course.					
The employee is showing a positive impact on behavior at work.					
Attending the course has had a positive impact on the employee/the business.					
The employee is demonstrating a sustained skill behavioral development in line with the course objectives.					
The employee talks with enthusiasm about the course.					

What impact has the program had on the business?
Note any further actions / development requirements in line with the course objectives.

Post-Course Reaction Score		Pre-Course Learning Score		Post-Course Learning Score		Manager Post-Course Effectiveness Score	

© *Greencore Group plc*

- Teams sorted out problems themselves, having had decision-making tasks truly delegated to them.
- Managers participating in the program worked cross-functionally to bring about positive changes in the business that would not have otherwise occurred.

- The team was to report to the executive team with updates on a bi-monthly basis. The challenge was met within six weeks and reversed a 20-week trend. The results have been consistent, with the variance staying within the predetermined standard for the last nine weeks. This represents a savings (or recovery) of over $250,000 so far.

Here are some quotes from program participants, providing insights into additional benefits:

- "By learning what motivates others, we are able to flex our behaviors according to what they need."
- "I realize how much money we burn not knowing the purpose of our meeting."
- "My lightbulb moment was the impact on others of my not really listening to them."
- "I've been using my time to give my team purpose and clarify critical success factors so that I can get stuff done."

A critical part of this program was the challenge set by the site's executive team, who for the first time were required to use the new learning to deliver through facilitation, teamwork, and stakeholder management. The challenges required problem solving, root cause analysis, and coaching, for example, to help the factory teams meet their forecasts, which they were struggling to do.

Due to the success of the pilot program, a second cohort of 12 managers was added.

Summary

Greencore has provided a good example of how to design a leadership development program so there are defined performance objectives and measurable outcomes. The combination of structure and participant ownership yielded both financial and human resource-related outcomes that benefit both the company and the individuals involved.

CHAPTER 18

Service Over and Above the Rest (SOAR) Program: Emirates Airline

Joyce Donohoe, Paul Beech, and Karen Bell-Wright

Founded in 1985, Emirates Airline is part of the Emirates Group, which employs more than 50,000 people. With its headquarters in Dubai, United Arab Emirates, the airline ranks among the top 10 airlines worldwide in revenue and passenger miles.

Figure 18-1. Emirates Airline Soars High

© *The Emirates Group*

The Emirates Group has its own learning and development unit, Emirates Group Learning and Development (GLD), which supports the majority of business units within the corporation. The GLD team was already aware that the service they provided added value to the organization, but often they did not have any tangible evidence to support this. The team believed that the application of the ADDIE training model, while fundamentally sound, required strengthening. In response, the GLD team, with the assistance of Kirkpatrick Partners, initiated an organization-wide transformation from a model of training and performance to one of business partnership.

To kick-start the process internally, a policy statement was created detailing GLD's approach to learning and performance. This policy statement formed the foundation for this strategy:

- We are learning and development professionals dedicated to helping employees at all levels enhance their individual performances, collectively leading to true competitive advantage.
- It is not enough to be a world-class training provider. Our employees and business partners deserve more.
- To become true strategic business partners, we need to identify and implement innovative, worldwide best practices while leveraging current core competencies.
- Learning is a process, not an event. Our purpose and our jobs extend beyond the walls of our training facility.
- Collaboration with business leaders at all levels will be critical to corporate success. Much of our work will include providing advice and support to those who have the power to enhance a culture that encourages ongoing learning and on-the-job application of training.
- A business-partnership approach to learning, performance, and results is the best way to maximize each initiative. This involves first building collaboration, internal bridges, and trust with our internal customers.
- It takes each of us to commit to our mission by being open to trying this new approach and working with a renewed emphasis on internal communication. This will be the key to our success.

While the airline is loved and admired for its innovative products and excellent service provided to customers on board its 235 aircraft fleet, it was important to ensure that this service was consistent across all Emirates customer touch points. Emirates Airline's Global Contact Center's Service Over and Above the Rest (SOAR) Program was selected to partner with GLD in this new approach for two reasons:

1. The two functional areas had a good history of working together, and the management team was open minded about undertaking this new learning and performance methodology.
2. This high-profile strategic program, once successfully executed, would set the stage for similar cooperative global initiatives.

Actions

The overall desired outcome of the SOAR program was to introduce a customer service intervention at all contact centers, which would provide a consistent personalized service focusing on customer service and growing sales. The goals were twofold: 1) to increase sales at the enterprise level by 20 percent to support the increase in capacity; and 2) to apply the new service style in 80 percent of all call centers, thereby improving the quality of calls.

The program was rolled out in Dubai (UAE), Mumbai (India), Melbourne (Australia), Manchester (U.K.), New York City (U.S.), and Guangzhou (China). In addition to the creation and implementation of two training programs for the leadership team and agents, a formalized on-the-job support and aligned performance package was created.

Pre-SOAR Preparation

Kirkpatrick business partnership principles were taught to key leaders from both the learning and business sides of the initiative:

- The end is the beginning.
- Return on expectations (ROE) is the ultimate indicator of value.
- Business partnership is necessary to bring about positive ROE.
- Value must be created before it can be demonstrated.
- A compelling chain of evidence demonstrates your bottom-line value.

Next, specific measures of success were determined, and the subsequent required level of effort was defined. A memorandum of understanding was drafted detailing key processes and roles, required drivers of critical on-the-job behaviors, and evaluation methodology.

SOAR and Coach for Performance Formal Training

The central learning objective in both programs was for team leaders and agents to apply a global service style (internally and externally). The SOAR program for agents focused on four key themes to improve the service experience and enhance relationship selling: 1) Recognize and Respect; 2) Calm and Assured; 3) Empathy and Warmth; and 4) Cosmopolitan. The Coach for Performance program taught the team leaders how to apply the new service style themes internally with their teams and coach and mentor their agents to continually apply the service style on calls.

Formalized on-the-Job Support

The business partnership model is grounded in the fact that training alone will not bring about significant performance and results. For the first time in Emirates Group history, these training programs were followed by an aligned performance management package focusing on monitoring, monthly dashboards, on-the-job training, recognition, role modeling, coaching, global calibrations of calls, and ongoing data analysis (Figure 18-2):

Figure 18-2. On-the-Job Support Elements

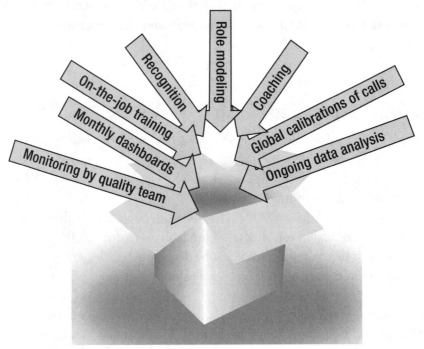

© *The Emirates Group*

This support enabled the agents to apply the new service behaviors as the program was rolled out. It also provided real-time data to the business on the improvements in the service experience.

The Evaluation and Reward Strategy

A process was created to collate and review monthly call-quality scores and sales figures. A leadership questionnaire was also created to evaluate application of the service style internally. Two recognition programs were created: "Shout-Out," for team leaders who were acting as positive role models, and "Agent of the Month," which recognized agents providing exemplary customer service and sales.

Results

The Coach for Performance program taught the team leaders how to apply the new service style internally with their teams. Here are the results of the questionnaire sent to the agents asking them how well their own team leaders were doing applying the service style with them (Figure 18-3). Each percentage shown is an average score of the responses received.

Figure 18-3. Results of Coach for Performance Questionnaire

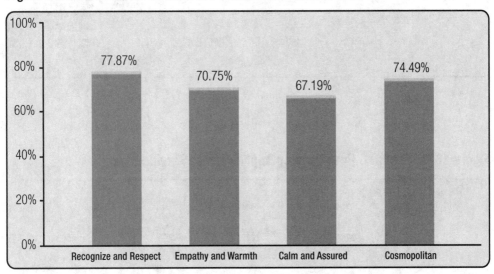

© *The Emirates Group*

Similarly, SOAR taught agents how to apply the service style externally with customers to improve the service experience and enhance relationship selling. The post-training survey showed an average of 94 percent of agents felt the program content was relevant to their jobs, and the Participant Reaction Survey indicated that the agents felt more knowledgeable, confident, and committed to apply the service style after the training (Figure 18-4).

The quality team monitored 13,366 phone conversations with customers, and the agents' application of the service style on calls pre- and post-training was measured (Figure 18-5).

Actual customer complaints also decreased during the period immediately after the SOAR program (Figure 18-6).

Figure 18-4. Post-Training Participant Reaction Survey

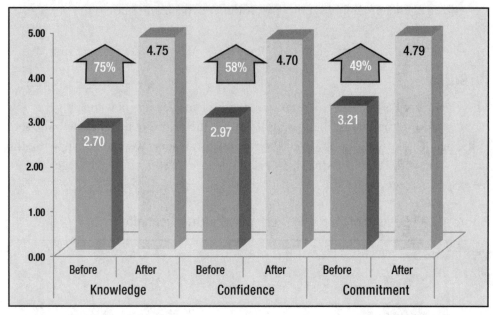

© *The Emirates Group*

Figure 18-5. Pre- and Post-Training Application of Service Style

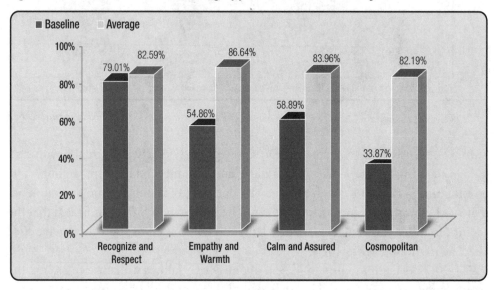

© *The Emirates Group*

Figure 18-6. Post-Training Customer Complaints

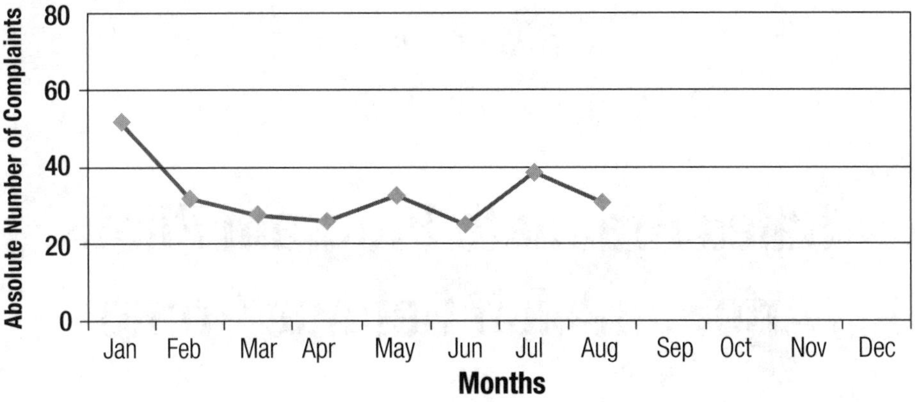

© *The Emirates Group*

Summary

The SOAR-GLD partnership has moved training beyond the walls of the classroom and into the organization, where both the business stakeholders and the L&D team worked together and today are able to celebrate their success. In this process, the GLD team has built credibility within the entire organization, developed stronger relationships, and continued to work with their business partners in a continual improvement process.

SOAR revolutionized the environment of the Global Contact Center by focusing the entire team on the customer. SOAR gave the center the global consistency that was needed and a change in internal culture whereby success at every level was measured, celebrated, and recognized.

Other organizations could benefit from the Emirates GLD learning—that maximum impact from L&D interventions happens when both the training team and the business work together to define clear goals, ensure the learning and performance package are intrinsically linked, and monitor progress.

The Emirates GLD team offers three recommendations to other organizations considering a training initiative to improve business outcomes: 1) prior to any mission-critical training initiative, meet with and draft a memorandum of understanding among all parties, spelling out critical roles and steps along the way; 2) offer a learning and performance package approach to any major business need as opposed to a training initiative; and 3) monitor critical behaviors and other important metrics during the execution stage of major initiatives and make adjustments along the way based on data that is not up to standard.

CHAPTER 19

Sales Graduate Program Pilot: ArjoHuntleigh Getinge Group

Linn Steer

ArjoHuntleigh—part of the Getinge Group—is a leading global provider of medical equipment for safe patient handling and hygiene, pressure ulcer and venous thromboembolism (VTE) prevention, and infection control. Its aims are improved clinical and financial outcomes as well as a safer environment for both patients and caregivers within the healthcare field.

Business Need and Program Intent

In accordance with developments in the global healthcare market, the customer buying ArjoHuntleigh equipment has changed—from a clinical manager buying single products on the ward level to a facility or management group buying complete solutions. Therefore, the account manager profile must adjust from being product to customer focused; that is, to understanding customer needs, determining how best to meet them, and appropriately communicating the corresponding solutions back to the customer.

Traditionally, ArjoHuntleigh hires experienced account managers who know the business well and can start selling from the first day. However, these managers often come straight from competition and are likely to have the same profile as our own sales people. Therefore, as part of a company-wide, strategic growth initiative to increase sales-force capabilities and sales effectiveness, the ArjoHuntleigh Academy piloted a European sales graduate program during 2014–2015. The aim was to bring a group of high potentials without experience through a high-intensity, accelerated learning program consisting of training boot camps combined with on-the-job training and real work.

Stakeholder Expectations

Apart from gaining clear evidence that the sales graduate program leads to the desired outcomes, stakeholder expectations were twofold: 1) to attract and develop a group of young, mobile, ambitious high potentials without previous experience who rapidly exhibit desired selling behavior; that is, are business minded with a good understanding of solution selling and our customer intimacy strategy, to reach a higher degree of proficiency in executive sales and analytically based, strategic sales; and 2) to ultimately develop an improved sales talent pipeline, including excellent candidates who can be promoted into various strategic sales and leadership positions, thereby contributing significantly to the overall company goal of increasing revenue organically by 18 percent by the end of 2019.

Project Methodology

The project methodology involved five steps:

1. **Idea generation and management approval:** The philosophy and rough program draft were generated by the corporate HR function.

2. **Market selection:** We decided to run the pilot program in Europe and include candidates from six of our biggest and most mature markets. The countries invited had to ensure sales territories for their candidates, sales management support (including dedicated coaches), and an HR partner to help with recruitment and personal development.

3. **Finding the right candidates:** After intense testing, including behavioral and motivational assessments, logical thinking, and a business case, individuals were selected and started their sales graduate journey together at the end of summer 2014.

4. **Program setup:** The academy designed and delivered an intense training program consisting of three two-week, instructor-led boot camps, preparation assignments, and follow-up work. The content included in the boot camps gave sales graduates a broad knowledge base. We introduced the company framework (strategy, organization, and company introduction, for example) early on and then added content from our sales certification curriculum to this throughout the program. In addition, special workshops providing deeper insights to different parts of our business, were conducted. The idea was to make learning more digestible and ensure that the

graduates got a solutions approach from the very start (the onion approach—peeling off one layer at a time).

After each boot camp, a follow-up conference call was set up with local HR managers and coaches to run through what the graduates had learned and how they could support them locally. In between each boot camp, the graduates took on-the-job training—for example, co-riding with experienced sales and service representatives, practicing cold calling, and learning the customer relationship management (CRM) system. The program ended with a two-day graduation workshop in July 2015.

5. **Support system:** A learning-transfer platform called Promote was used to drive and monitor progress throughout the program. Having the graduates, coaches, and facilitators connected through one system made program management quite easy. We also set up program targets that the graduates would update during the program along with their own personal goals.

Evaluation Approach

Level 1 Reaction was measured continuously using instructor observation, pulse checks, and individual interviews. After each boot camp, the different sessions were ranked within the group, and there were participant discussions about how and why they voted the way they did (top 3 and bottom 3). Formal feedback forms were also used for all sessions included in the sales certification curriculum (Table 19-1).

In addition to the graduates' input, Blended Evaluation® surveys (L1- L4) were also sent out and filled in by their managers; these gave us a very good understanding of the graduates' engagement, relevance, and satisfaction.

Level 2 evaluation was conducted before, during, and after the boot camps. Knowledge was evaluated through online exams prior to classroom training, ensuring that the graduates had gained a sufficient level after completing their preparation work. Their skills were observed and evaluated during class participation, role plays, case-study presentations, and product demonstrations, as well as teach backs and sales-call evaluations in the field (assessed by their line manager or coach). Attitude, confidence, and commitment were evaluated during discussions in class, individual interviews, and as part of our formal feedback form.

Level 3 Behavior information was gathered through the previously mentioned Blended Evaluation surveys and performance ratings using a general company performance review template sent out to managers by e-mail (Tables 19-2 and 19-3). This performance review evaluated the graduates on both individual targets and achievements against "SMART" principles ("what" was achieved), as well as "how" the individual performed against the company's behavioral cornerstones.

Table 19-1. Training Feedback Form

ArjoHuntleigh Academy — Training Feedback Form

Course:	

Course date(s):		Venue:	

Name:	

Company Name:		Dept./ Job title:	

	Please mark the number for each question that matches the corresponding smiley:	☹	🙁	🙂	😀
1	How well were the course objectives (described prior to the course) met?	1	2	3	4
2	How would you rate your level of confidence regarding the covered topics *before* the training & pre-training?	1	2	3	4
3	How would you rate your level of confidence regarding the covered topics *after* the training & pre-training?	1	2	3	4
4	How would you rate the relevance of the pre-training content*? *e-learning, assignments, documents/links etc. sent out to prepare for classroom training	n/a 1	2	3	4
5	How would you rate the overall course structure*? *The way of transmission and order of topics	1	2	3	4
6	How relevant was the course to your job?	1	2	3	4
7	How would you rate the venue and facilities?	1	2	3	4
8	What is your overall impression of the course?	1	2	3	4

9	Please rate the following per trainer/presenter from 1 to 4:	☹=1	🙁=2	🙂=3	😀=4

	Trainer A:	Trainer B:	Trainer C:	Trainer D:	Trainer E:
Name(s) of trainer/presenter(s):					
Trainer delivery style:					
Trainer knowledge:					
Trainer's course content:					
Ability & willingness to answer questions:					
Overall trainer rating:					

10	What were your personal reasons/objectives for attending this course?
11	Which parts of the course did you find most valuable? Why?
12	How will this training be used in your work?
13	Do you have any suggestions how we can improve the course?
14	Has the training raised any additional training needs or resource requirements?
15	Would you recommend this course to others? YES NO
16	Additional comments:

© *ArjoHuntleigh Getinge Group*

Table 19-2. Graduate Scheme Manager / Mentor Survey

Graduate Name	
Employing Country	
Line Manager / Coach Name	

1. Please assess the overall success and impact your graduate has made to your business areas.

2. How well do you think the boot camps have equipped your graduate(s) for the work they have been required to undertake? Have they "added value" in the workplace compared to existing employees who haven't had such development opportunities?

3. What specific areas do you feel would be added value within the boot camps if a similar scheme was used in the future?

4. What impact did the "two-week intensive" format of the boot camps have on your business area?

5. Please assess the impact of the graduate's being away from the business area for the boot camps on "lost sales." If you are able to quantify this impact, also indicate this.

6. Do you have any suggestions that could improve the format of the boot camps in future years to minimize the impact on your business area?

7. Has the format enabled you to attract a higher caliber of salesperson compared to standard recruitment processes?

8. If you had the opportunity (budget constraints permitting), would you be interested in taking graduates through a similar program in the future? (If "no," please explain; your feedback will enable us to adapt the program in the future.)

9. Please provide us with any other feedback you feel may be of benefit in assessing this program.

Thank you for taking the time to complete this questionnaire.

Table 19-3. Performance Appraisal Discussion 2014

Employee's Name		Employee's Title	
Supervisor's Name		Supervisor's Title	
Location		Performance Period	From (date): To (date):

Please refer to the "Manager's Performance Appraisal Review and Performance Development Plan (PDP) planning guide" for full guidance on how to complete this form.

Managers and employees have previously agreed objectives for the rating period based on key performance indicators of the role. Provide both constructive and positive feedback on how these employee achievements can be seen in the employee's overall performance.

Within the Getinge Group we have set Cornerstone Behaviors and Core Competencies. This feedback in the two sections below must therefore refer to our Cornerstone Behaviors and Core Competency requirements at all times.

A. Individual Targets

Specific Target against "SMART" principles	"What" was accomplished	"What" Rating
		Choose an item.
		Choose an item.
		Choose an item.
		Choose an item.

Rating ("What")	Rating Average
	Choose an item.

B. "How" has the individual performed against our Behavioral Cornerstones?

Rating ("How")	Rating Average
	Choose an item.

Overall combined Rating ("What" + "How")	Rating Average
	Choose an item.

Table 19-3. Performance Appraisal Discussion 2014 *(continued)*

C. Employee Comments

D. Manager Summary

E. Signatures			
Date			
Signature			
Print Name			
	EMPLOYEE	IMMEDIATE SUPERVISOR	NEXT LEVEL MANAGER

© *ArjoHuntleigh Getinge Group*

The graduates also completed an online survey during the final graduation work-shop, in which they explained how they had applied their learnings from the boot camps in the field and rated the importance or contribution of the different aspects of the graduate program (success factors) (Table 19-4). Managers also conducted sales-call evaluations with the graduates.

Level 4 evaluation of leading indicators was conducted primarily with help from sales managers, as we had challenges retrieving data from the CRM system. The manager Blended Evaluation survey, combined with actual sales data retrieved from each market, the managers' mapping of their graduates using a top talent and succession template and a nine-box talent grid, feedback from the graduates, and a customer testimonial indicated that the program was working as intended (Tables 19-5 and 19-6).

Table 19-4. Sales Graduate Program—Application and Impact Evaluation

PROMOTE

1. To what extent has PROMOTE helped you prepare for the boot camps?
   a. Not at all (we would do just as well/better without it)
   b. A little
   c. Quite a lot
   d. It has been crucial
   Comments:

2. To what extent has PROMOTE helped you reflect on your learning after the boot camps?
   a. Not at all (we would do just as well/better without it)
   b. A little
   c. Quite a lot
   d. It has been crucial
   Comments:

3. To what extent has PROMOTE helped you interact with your coach?
   a. Not at all (we would do just as well/better without it)
   b. A little
   c. Quite a lot
   d. It has been crucial
   Comments:

4. How easy was it for you to learn how to use PROMOTE?
   a. Really difficult
   b. A little difficult
   c. Quite easy
   d. Very easy and intuitive
   Comments:

5. How easy was it for your coach to learn how to use PROMOTE?
   a. Really difficult
   b. A little difficult
   c. Quite easy
   d. Very easy and intuitive
   Comments:

PROGRAM CONTRIBUTION

6. Please rate the level of importance/contribution of the below factors in your job and success so far:
   a. The boot camp selling skills training (AECM, AKAM, Diligent case study)
   b. The boot camp product training
   c. The boot camp presentation skills & PAR training
   d. The Insights Discovery Profile (color assessment)
   e. PROMOTE
   f. My coach
   g. The other graduates
   h. Local colleagues
   i. Field work (learning on the job)
   j. Local training (please specify type of training in comment field below)
   k. The boot camp venues (meeting people and seeing the factory, head office, etc.)

Table 19-4. Sales Graduate Program—Application and Impact Evaluation *(continued)*

l. My own motivation and ambition
m. Other (please specify below)

Ratings: Not important at all – A little important – Important – Very important / invaluable
Comments:

7. Please rate the level of estimated importance/contribution of the below factors on your success in the future:
   a. The boot camp selling skills training (AECM, AKAM, Diligent case study)
   b. The boot camp product training
   c. The boot camp presentation skills & PAR training
   d. The Insights Discovery Profile (color assessment)
   e. PROMOTE
   f. My coach
   g. The other graduates
   h. Local colleagues
   i. Field work (learning on the job)
   j. Local training (please specify type of training in comment field below)
   k. The boot camp venues (meeting people and seeing the factory, head office, etc.)
   l. My own motivation and ambition
   m. Other (please specify below)

   Ratings: Not important at all – A little important – Important – Very important / invaluable
   Comments:

ALIGNMENT and ENGAGEMENT

8. How aligned and engaged do you feel the Global L&P Director has been during the program?
   a. Not at all
   b. A little
   c. Quite a lot
   d. Totally aligned and engaged
   Comments:

9. How aligned and engaged do you feel the boot camp trainers have been during the program?
   a. Not at all
   b. A little
   c. Quite a lot
   d. Totally aligned and engaged
   Comments:

10. How aligned and engaged do you feel your local HR partner/manager has been during the program?
    a. Not at all
    b. A little
    c. Quite a lot
    d. Totally aligned and engaged
    Comments:

11. How aligned and engaged do you feel your line manager/coach has been during the program?
    a. Not at all
    b. A little
    c. Quite a lot
    d. Totally aligned and engaged
    Comments:

Table 19-4. Sales Graduate Program—Application and Impact Evaluation *(continued)*

12. How aligned and engaged do you feel your local sales management has been during the program?
    a. Not at all
    b. A little
    c. Quite a lot
    d. Totally aligned and engaged

    Comments:

APPLICATION OF LEARNING

Please give three examples of how you have used your learnings from the boot camps in your job and what effect it had (e.g., AECM, AKAM, PAR/Presentation skills, Insights Discovery Profile, product or clinical knowledge, corporate knowledge—strategy, how other departments/functions work, etc.):

13. Application example 1:

14. Application example 2:

15. Application example 3:

PROGRAM SETUP

16. If you joined the company without taking part in the sales graduate program, what impact would that have on your job and success (with the current local structure and onboarding process)?
    a. Positive impact (I would have done better without the sales graduate program)
    b. No impact (I would have reached the same place I am in)
    c. Little impact (I would not really be where I am now but not too far off)
    d. Quite high impact (I would definitely not be where I am now)
    e. Very high impact (I would not be close to where I am now)

    Comments:

17. If you joined the company and took part in a local sales graduate program (only participants from your country), what impact would that have on your job and success (with the same content but with local adaptation and no international travel)?
    a. Positive impact (I would have done better doing this locally)
    b. No impact (I would have reached the same place I am in)
    c. Little impact (I would not really be where I am now but not too far off)
    d. Quite high impact (I would definitely not be where I am now)
    e. Very high impact (I would not be close to where I am now)

    Comments:

18. Please share any additional reflections or comments on content, structure, application, engagement, alignment, etc.:

Table 19-5. Top Talent and Succession Overview

Name	Location	Function/ Department	Current Position	Geographic Mobility	Language Skills	Language Ability Level	Why High Potential? Describe Key Success Factors

Short-Term Position Goal (Please indicate if Ready Now or will be ready in the Short Term—1–3 years)	Mid-Term Position Goal (3–5 years)	Long-Term Position Goal (5 Years +)	Competency Strengths	Competency Development Needs	Other Areas for Development

Table 19-6. Sales Graduate Talent Grid

		Performance →		
		Below	**Meets**	**Exceeds**
Potential →	**High (2 levels)**	Needs Coaching	Emerging Talent	Outstanding Talent
	Promotable (1 level)	Questionable Performer	Solid Contributor	Outstanding Contributor
	Low	Under Performer	Solid Performer	Outstanding Performer

© *ArjoHuntleigh Getinge Group*

Key Level 3 Findings

Performance ratings by line managers after nine months showed that all graduates had either met or exceeded their expectations, which were to establish relationships with customers, deliver compelling presentations, and close sales. Our manager survey also showed desired graduate behavior in the field.

The online survey completed by the graduates at the graduation workshop showed how they had applied their learnings from the boot camps in the field. Here are some examples:

Before getting to know the colors in the Insights Discovery Profile I had an appointment with a customer and it was one of my worst-ever meetings. After I knew about the colors it was much clearer why, and I knew that it would maybe be better to adapt myself to him and in which way. This knowledge really helped me to establish a better relationship.

Presentation skills are also something I feel I use every day. It's not just about standing up in front of customers and going through slides or interactive presentations, even when you sit one-to-one going through products and services this is also a kind of presentation, just on a smaller level. Because of our extra training and support around presenting, I feel like I am able to keep my customers' concentration and keep them interactive with what I am discussing.

Last December, I had a meeting with a potentially new customer. She wanted to buy three bath systems, so it was for me the first opportunity I had to fully follow all the AECM [ArjoHuntleigh Effective Call Management] steps— from the AH presentation (positive 8 . . .) to the moment when I convinced her to buy the Rhapsody P220 with the options her facility needed.

The AECM training has been particularly useful when it comes to managing obstacles. This is a quite common situation for me and it is thanks to that training that I am able to deal properly with obstacles.

I have used AKAM [ArjoHuntleigh Key Account Management] to help with my customer development not only to benefit the customer, but also to make sure that I am working closely with my colleagues and to make sure that we all have the same goal.

Key Level 4 Findings

Although it is too early to evaluate the results fully, some leading indicators show we are on the right track:

1. **Global sales certification:** All candidates had the ability to become fully certified account managers.
2. **Opportunities and orders to prioritized accounts:** Since some countries have not yet implemented the global CRM system, it has been difficult to pull out this data. Manager feedback does, however, indicate that the graduates are approaching the right accounts, and the order intake during the program is impressive.
3. **Solution sales:** Managers' survey input indicates that the sales graduates are solutions oriented in their sales approach, although we have had some trouble verifying this.
4. **Strong career potential and promotions:** Talent mapping by managers shows strong career potential. On the nine-box talent grid, four of the eight graduates are considered "emerging talents," three are "outstanding

contributors," and one is a "solid contributor." In addition, two graduates have already been promoted, one to a sales excellence and CRM manager role, and the other to a key account manager role, along with having become a local selling skills trainer.

5. **Employee engagement and customer satisfaction:** Apart from managers saying the graduates are "great with customers" in the manager survey, one of the graduate's line managers received the following e-mail:

> *Dear Ian,*
>
> *I write to you regarding Danielle, our account manager. Late last year I was trying desperately to get in contact with our account manager as our account was a bit of a mess. After some time Danielle was introduced to us. She came to meet us and took on the challenge of our account and of me, and I admit I was very frustrated. Danielle has worked incredibly hard to iron out the process with us, and has enabled us to ensure the workings of the account are in check, i.e., a password on the account, account numbers, and contacts for both parties.*
>
> *We had a number of hire items that I was advised were lost by ward staff. Danielle offered to visit the units in question to check the equipment with me. On this visit Danielle was great. Her product knowledge was amazing and she really shone. Not only did she assist with tracking down the items on hire, she was able to provide guidance on the existing owned equipment on the ward. Danielle observed the patients on the units and advised us on other products that are far more suitable for their needs. I have been able to take these suggested products on to the Trust, who are happy to trial the equipment. Her guidance on the existing products has been well received also.*
>
> *She has really turned things around so much so I feel compelled to email you. This level of care, attention, and perseverance is rarely seen. In all honesty, Danielle is a shining example of an account manager. What a wonderful asset to your team. Danielle, I cannot thank you enough.*
>
> *Kind regards,*
> *Procurement Officer, NHS Trust*

6. **Program acceptance:** Survey results from sales managers, together with verbal feedback from country managers and HR leaders, confirm that the sales graduate program pilot was perceived as very successful. They all want the program to continue so they can give the same opportunity to future talents and thereby strengthen their organizations even further.

Success Factors

The graduates rated the importance or contribution of the different aspects of the current graduate program (Table 19-7).

Table 19-7. Success Factor Contribution

Please rate the level of importance/contribution of the below factors in your job and success so far:

Item	Rating Average
The other graduates	4.00
My own motivation and ambition	3.88
The boot camp selling skills training (AECM, AKAM, Diligent case study)	3.75
The boot camp presentations skills and PAR training	3.63
Field work (learning on the job)	3.63
My coach	3.50
The boot camp venues (meeting people and seeing the factory, head office, etc.)	3.50
The Insight Discovery Profile (color assessment)	3.43
The boot camp product training	3.38
Local colleagues	3.25
PROMOTE	3.13
Local training (please specify type of training in comment field below)	2.88

Ratings are based on a 4-point scale, with 4 being the highest level of importance/greatest contribution.

© *ArjoHuntleigh Getinge Group*

Recommendations

For future academy programs, recommendations focus on all three areas: before, during, and after training. Prior to training, recommendations point to the importance of having local support in place before training begins:

- Train coaches in their roles prior to starting the program.
- Get stronger local commitment through a joint start-up meeting, run through Promote with sales management prior to inviting the graduates.
- Provide local HR with their own Promote login to make it easier for them to follow the program (no suitable role available at present but hopefully in the future).
- Connect the graduates with suitable mentors outside of the local organization.
- Allow existing employees with great potential to apply for this program.

To made adjustments during training, recommendations focus on the need for flexibility, to be able to quickly modify the program to the specific needs and talents of participants as well as the organization:

- Extend the program from 12 to 18 months to allow more time for undisturbed learning, practicing cold calling, and international exchange, for example.
- Place one of the boot camps in a country that is "walking the talk" and has the ability to add more inspirational topics and facilitators.
- Add a strategic project assignment that runs throughout the program.
- Use our alumni graduates as "program buddies."
- Involve more local sales people who can serve as inspiration.
- Involve customers who can give their perspective on us.

Post-training recommendations ensure continued follow-up of the program results and the individual development of the graduates:

- Have follow-up surveys for graduates ready before the graduation workshop.
- Once everyone is on the same CRM system, make a dashboard that enables simple follow-up on graduates' results (for example, order intake, sales to prioritized accounts, and solution sales).
- Involve the graduates in incubator projects and similar activities to utilize their fresh ideas and keep them alert and inspired.

Summary

The sales graduate pilot program has proven that it is possible to bring a group of high potentials without experience through a high-intensity, accelerated learning program and turn them into successful customer- and solutions-oriented account managers. All the participating countries want to run this program again, and all of them are happy with the program and their graduates.

CHAPTER 20

Accident Reduction Program: Maryland Transit Administration

Michael Wiedecker

The Maryland Transit Administration (MTA) is a division of the Maryland Department of Transportation, and one of the largest multimodal transit systems in the United States. The MTA system includes local and commuter bus, light rail, Metro subway, Maryland Area Regional Commuter (MARC) Train Service, and a comprehensive paratransit (mobility) system. The mission of MTA is "Providing safe, efficient, and reliable transit across Maryland with world-class customer service."

In July 2012, soon after MTA increased bus operator hiring, there was a significant increase in accidents of new bus operators. These operators are defined as those with less than one year of experience after graduating from the 10-week bus operator training program. Upon cursory review, MTA did not note any significant changes in the training programs to explain the rash of accidents. The same instructors continued to do the instructing, the training material was not changed, the tests remained the same, the use of the bus simulator continued, and instructors still conducted efficiency ride checks as they always had. Management was thus faced with a puzzling and serious problem that was affecting the cost of operations due to the increased expense of bus repairs, worker compensation claims, overtime costs, higher and more frequent insurance payouts, and the inevitable impact on the accomplishment of MTA's mission.

MTA, in partnership with PTG International, a small business dedicated to applying web and computer-based technologies to the automated assessment of performance and to the evaluation of training, decided to analyze bus operations data to search for links and correlations that could point to the reasons why the MTA's new bus operators were experiencing a high rate of accidents within one year of graduation, and then resolve the issues.

There were five goals set by the team at the outset:

Goal #1—New Bus Operator Accident Reduction

- Increase the percentage of new bus operators who do not attend post-accident training (PAT) within three months of graduation by 25 percent.
- Increase the percentage of new bus operators who do not attend PAT within three to six months of graduation by 20 percent.
- Have a new bus operator class where no one attends a PAT within six months of graduating.

Goal #2—Reduce the number of times any bus operator repeats PAT.

Goal #3—Conduct a data-driven review of new bus operator training, comparing key training measurements with accident rates to determine if there is a link between training content, methodology, impact, and the accident rate.

Goal #4—Examine new operator recruiting practices to determine if there is any connection between pre-employment hiring practices and downstream performance of each bus operator.

Goal #5—Change any existing practices, if indicated, such as the content, structure, and length of the training, including how performance reviews of new professional bus operators were conducted and documented during training and after graduation.

Project Methodology

The Kirkpatrick Business Partnership Model and a dynamic training dashboard (provided by PTG International) are the cornerstones of this project. The operations training team also wanted to become more than just training partners; they wanted to be business partners in assisting other departments within MTA achieve their expected business outcomes.

MTA recognized that they needed to do more than just send as many employees as they could, and as fast as they could, through training classes. To assess overall goal attainment and achievement of expectations, they needed to evaluate training on all four Kirkpatrick levels. If they failed to objectively measure training, how would they know if their training programs were supporting MTA or becoming an obstacle?

Required Drivers

MTA knew not to rely on training alone to accomplish its goals and contribute to its mission. Therefore, a number of actions immediately following the conclusion of the programs and in the months to follow were put into practice to drive and maximize on-the-job application and results.

- **Monitoring:** Efficiency ride checks using checklists, a 90-day probationary period, points system, and a performance dashboard
- **Reinforcing:** Rite of passage ceremony, passing the baton ceremony, graduate ceremony, "We'll always be there for you" program, rule book, and other job aids
- **Encouraging:** Certified union mentors, supervisor coaches, including opportunities for bus operators to reach out to instructors
- **Rewarding:** Opportunity to become a union instructor or mentor, MTA Facebook recognition.

Evaluation Methodology

MTA administered a 60-question final exam at the end of the program. An immediate post-course evaluation was implemented to collect post-training data (Table 20-1).

MTA implemented a Level 2 observation checklist completed by instructors as they observe bus operator candidates' behind-the-wheel performance during their initial 10 weeks of training (Table 20-2).

MTA also implemented a Level 3 observation checklist in which instructors perform ride-along evaluations of a bus operator's knowledge and skills after graduation (Table 20-3). Bus operations instructors also used this form to evaluate professional bus operators during post-accident training (PAT). After completing a bus operator performance report, the instructor meets with the operator, discusses the findings one-on-one, and makes recommendations regarding the operator's performance, including additional training if needed. These results are also shared with the stakeholders of bus management staff.

For Level 4 data, MTA operations training took existing accident frequency data from PAT attendance records and entered this data into their learning management system (LMS). When a bus operator is involved in a preventable accident, MTA requires that the professional bus operator attend PAT shortly after the accident, usually within two weeks. So, the length of time between the training graduation date (Grad) and the first PAT was recorded to determine when the new bus operator was involved in his or her first accident.

Table 20-1. End-of-Course Evaluation Form

MARYLAND TRANSIT ADMINISTRATION
Level 1 End-of-Course Evaluation
Instructor-Led Training

* Use a No. 2 pencil or black pen only.
* Make solid marks that fill the circle completely.
* Do not fold, tear or mutilate this form.
The ONLY correct mark... ●

Course Title: _____

Date(s): ___ ___ ___ / ___ ___ ___   Facility: _____
         mo day yr   mo day yr

Please indicate your level of agreement with each of the following statements.
1 = Strongly Disagree   2 = Disagree   3 = Agree   4 = Strongly Agree

Preparation
1. My manager and I set expectations for learning prior to the course.   ① ② ③ ④

Relevance
2. The content covered in this course is relevant and applicable to my job.   ① ② ③ ④
3. This course will help me to improve my job performance.   ① ② ③ ④
4. I believe it will be worth my effort to apply what I learned to work.   ① ② ③ ④

Course Content
5. The course materials aided in my learning.   ① ② ③ ④
6. The course length was sufficient for the amount of content.   ① ② ③ ④
7. The course content was appropriate for my experience/skill level.   ① ② ③ ④
8. The tests were consistent with the course content.   ① ② ③ ④

Course Learning Activities
9. The learning activities helped to reinforce what I was taught in the class.   ① ② ③ ④
10. Participation and interaction among participants were encouraged.   ① ② ③ ④
11. The variety of presentation methods contributed to my level of engagement.   ① ② ③ ④

Training Environment
12. The training environment was conducive to my learning experience.   ① ② ③ ④

Alignment / Commitment
13. I am confident that I can apply what I learned to my job.   ① ② ③ ④
14. I am committed to using the knowledge, awareness, and/or skills I learned to do my job.   ① ② ③ ④

Learning Style Preference
15. I learn best when the content is presented to me in the following format: Ⓗ Hands-On
    Select ONLY one.   Ⓦ Written Text
    Ⓒ Combination of the above

Please continue your evaluation on the back.

Table 20-1. End-of-Course Evaluation Form *(continued)*

MARYLAND TRANSIT ADMINISTRATION	Instructor A	Instructor B
Level 1 End-of-Course Evaluation Instructor-Led Training		

Write in the four-digit instructor code for each instructor and then fill in the corresponding numbers. Please also print the instructor's name(s) below.

Instructor A: _____

Instructor B: _____

Please indicate your level of agreement with each of the following statements.
1 = Strongly Disagree   2 = Disagree   3 = Agree   4 = Strongly Agree

Instructors

	Instructor A	Instructor B
16. The presentation style of the instructor helped me to learn.	① ② ③ ④	① ② ③ ④
17. The instructor demonstrated subject matter expertise.	① ② ③ ④	① ② ③ ④
18. The instructor was prepared and organized.	① ② ③ ④	① ② ③ ④
19. The instructor was responsive to participant needs and questions.	① ② ③ ④	① ② ③ ④
20. The instructor effectively related the subject matter to my on-the-job application.	① ② ③ ④	① ② ③ ④

Please indicate your level of satisfaction with each of the following statements.
1 = Very Dissatisfied   2 = Dissatisfied   3 = Satisfied   4 = Very Satisfied

Course Overall Ratings

21. The content, overall.	① ② ③ ④
22. The materials, overall.	① ② ③ ④
23. The instructor(s), overall.	① ② ③ ④
24. The course, overall.	① ② ③ ④

Comments

What knowledge or skill(s) presented in this course will be most helpful once back on the job?

What barriers to applying what you learned can you anticipate?

Please share any other comments or recommendations you may have for improving this course.

Thank you for completing this evaluation. Your feedback is important!

MTA L1 Rev. 1.0.3, © 2012, PTG International, Inc.

Table 20-2. Bus Operator Candidate Evaluation Form

Bus Operator Candidate Training

Directions: Instructor, complete a Candidate Evaluation Form for each Candidate:
- At the end of each day (as an overall summary of the day's training)
- At the end of training program (Final Evaluation)

Candidate Name	Division	Badge No.	Payroll No.
Time On: Time Off:	Location On:	Location Off:	
Instructor Name	Today's Date	Miscellaneous Notes:	

Critical Safety Errors (On page 2, explain all checked factors.)

___Failed to stop at red light   ___Did not wear seatbelt   ___Failed to yield to pedes-
___Struck fixed object/vehicle   ___Accelerated in approach   trian in the crosswalk
___Failed to complete a pre-   of a yellow light   ___Other
    trip inspection   ___Cell phone/Electronic
                device usage

Factors to be Rated (Explain all Unsatisfactory ratings on page 2)

1. **STARTING:**
   ___NO ERRORS (SATISFACTORY)
   ___UNSATISFACTORY
       ___Fails to cover brake when starting the bus
       ___Fails to close front door before pulling off
       ___Makes false starts
       ___Allows bus to drift back
       ___Fails to check left & right sides before
           moving bus

2. **STOPPING:**
   ___NO ERRORS (SATISFACTORY)
   ___UNSATISFACTORY
       ___Fails to make complete stop at stop sign
       ___Improper application of brake
       ___Sudden stopping

3. **OBSERVATIONS:**
   ___NO ERRORS (SATISFACTORY)
   ___UNSATISFACTORY
       ___Incorrect mirror adjustment
       ___Fails to check mirrors every 3-5 seconds
       ___Stares or does not distribute attention
       ___Does not make adjustments for blind spots
       ___Fails to maintain 3-foot clearance

4. **FOLLOWING MOVING TRAFFIC**
   ___NO ERRORS (SATISFACTORY)
   ___UNSATISFACTORY
       ___Follows too closely, stops too close
       ___Fails to allow 10 feet when stopped
           behind vehicles
       ___Does not adjust for slow or passing
           vehicle

5. **RIGHT TURNS:**
   ___NO ERRORS (SATISFACTORY)
   ___UNSATISFACTORY
       ___Does not perform proper observations
       ___Positions bus improperly
       ___Turns from or into wrong lane
       ___Fails to maintain proper clearance
       ___Fails to coordinate speed & steering
       ___Exceeds 5 mph during turn

6. **CHANGING LANES, PASSING, BEING PASSED:**
   ___NO ERRORS (SATISFACTORY)
   ___UNSATISFACTORY
       ___Improper observations/clearance
       ___Fails to merge smoothly
       ___Fails to keep bus under full control
       ___Operates unsafely with traffic alongside
           bus
       ___Fails to close off right side properly

7. **INTERSECTION OPERATION:**
   ___NO ERRORS (SATISFACTORY)
   ___UNSATISFACTORY
       ___Accelerates to make yellow lights
       ___Fails to have bus under full control
       ___Fails to make L-R-L observations

8. **SCHOOL ZONES:**
   ___NO ERRORS (SATISFACTORY)
   ___UNSATISFACTORY
       ___Exceeds 5 mph in school bus zone
       ___Exceeds school zone speed limit

Office of Operations Training June 2013 Revised on April 27, 2015

Table 20-2. Bus Operator Candidate Evaluation Form *(continued)*

Explanation of any Safety or Unsatisfactory Ratings:

Positive Comments and/or Instructions/Recommendations Given to the Candidate:

This Evaluation is a: _____End of each Day   _____End of Training/Final

Check Overall Evaluation: _____*Satisfactory*   _____*Unsatisfactory*

Signatures: Instructor _____

Candidate _____

Office of Operations Training June 2013 Revised on April 27, 2015

Table 20-3. Bus Operator Performance Evaluation Form

Name:	Division:	Badge No.	Payroll No.	Date:

___Return To Duty ___Post- Accident ___Remedial	Bus No.	Run Number- Line- Block-

___Efficiency ___Follow Up	Time On	Place On
___Other:	Time Off	Place Off

Critical Safety Errors (On page 2, explain all checked factors.)

___Failed to stop at red light   ___Did not wear seatbelt   ___Cell phone/Electronic
___Struck fixed object/vehicle   ___Accelerated in approach of   device usage
___Failed to complete a pre-   a yellow light   ___Failed to yield to pedes-
trip inspection   trian in the crosswalk

Operating Skills

Observe and record each __Standard Operating Procedure__ (SOP) maneuver. Record each incorrect or unsafe maneuver. See Performance Rating Key On The Left Bottom Of Page Two (2).

STARTING:
___Fails to cover brake when starting the bus
___Fails to close front door before pulling off
___Makes false starts
___Allows bus to drift back
___Fails to check left & right sides before moving the bus
___SATISFACTORY   ___UNSATISFACTORY

STOPPING:
___Fails to make complete stop at stop sign
___Improper application of brake
___Sudden stopping
___SATISFACTORY   ___UNSATISFACTORY

OBSERVATIONS:
___Incorrect mirror adjustment
___Fails to check mirrors every 3-5 seconds
___Stares or does not distribute attention
___Does not make adjustments for blind spots
___Fails to maintain 3-foot clearance
___SATISFACTORY   ___UNSATISFACTORY

FOLLOWING MOVING TRAFFIC:
___Follows too closely, stops too close
___Fails to allow 10 feet when stopped behind vehicles
___Does not adjust for slow or passing vehicle
___SATISFACTORY   ___UNSATISFACTORY

LEFT TURNS:
___Does not perform proper observations
___Positions bus improperly
___Turns from or into wrong lane
___Fails to maintain proper clearance
___Fails to coordinate speed & steering
___Exceeds 5 mph during turn
___SATISFACTORY   ___UNSATISFACTORY

RIGHT TURNS:
___Does not perform proper observations
___Positions bus improperly
___Turns from or into wrong lane
___Fails to maintain proper clearance
___Fails to coordinate speed & steering
___Exceeds 5 mph during turn
___SATISFACTORY   ___UNSATISFACTORY

CHANGING LANES, PASSING, BEING PASSED:
___Improper observations/clearance
___Fails to merge smoothly
___Fails to keep bus under full control
___Operates unsafely with traffic alongside bus
___Fails to close off right side properly
___SATISFACTORY   ___UNSATISFACTORY

INTERSECTION OPERATION:
___Accelerates to make lights
___Fails to have bus under full control
___Fails to make L-R-L observations
___SATISFACTORY   ___UNSATISFACTORY

SERVICE STOPS:
___Approaches stops too fast
___Opens doors before bus stops
___Fails to stop 6-12" and parallel
___Stops in unsafe places
___Positions bus improperly at bus stops
___Fails to check right side for customers before moving
___Fails to monitor rear overhang
___Fails to watch doors as they open and close
___SATISFACTORY   ___UNSATISFACTORY

SCHOOL ZONES:
___Exceeds 5 mph in school bus zone
___Exceeds school zone speed limit
___SATISFACTORY   ___UNSATISFACTORY

Office of Operations Training October 13, 2013 Revised on June 16, 2015

Table 20-3. Bus Operator Performance Evaluation Form *(continued)*

Note: All Unsatisfactory ratings must be explained in detail below:

Explanation of Unsatisfactory Ratings:

Instructions Given:

Recommendations:

Performance Rating Key	**Overall Performance Rating**
○ Requires only 1 of safety critical = unsatisfactory	
○ Requires 2 or more unsatisfactory ratings for one factor of the same error = unsatisfactory	____ **Satisfactory**
○ Number of errors adds to 2 within a skill = unsatisfactory	
○ Number of errors across skills up to 4 or more = unsatisfactory	____ **Unsatisfactory**
○ Zero errors = Exceptional	____ **Exceptional**
Instructor's Signature	Operator's Signature
_____	_____

In addition, the size of each new bus operator class was studied, as well as the time the employees spent in behind-the-wheel training. Operations training also monitored what percentage of all MTA bus operators repeated PAT (Table 20-4).

Table 20-4. Number of Drivers Repeating PAT and Percentages

Number of PATs Attended	Number of Operators	Percent of Total PATs Attended
1	472	64.66%
2	178	24.38%
3	59	8.08%
4	15	2.05%
5	6	0.82%
Total	730	100.00%

© MTA

Key Findings and Results

The Level 1 data clearly indicated that the employees rated the training experience high in each of the categories except preparation. It was concluded from studying and analyzing the data that larger class sizes, inadequate instructor-to-student ratios, and reduced behind-the-wheel training time were the primary causes of an increase in accidents within 12 months of graduation. Bus operators were completing their training without enough driving experience to enhance their ability to recognize the development of potential accident scenarios and prevent accidents. As a result, any cost savings that MTA experienced by increasing the class size and putting more bus operators on the street was eliminated by the costs of the increased numbers of accidents.

A recommendation was made to MTA executive management to limit the class sizes to 15 students while maintaining an instructor to bus operator student ratio of one to three. Maintaining this ratio would ensure that each bus operator would receive the individualized attention and adequate behind-the-wheel training time to avoid and prevent accidents after graduation.

In 2015, the MTA executive team decided to hire a group of 30 new bus operators every month, a quadrupling in operations training production. It was agreed that 20 MTA professional bus operators would serve as union instructors to assist the operations training department with these larger and more frequent classes to maintain the ideal instructor-to-student ratio. Even with these larger class sizes and maintaining the instructor-to-student ratio, the graduating classes in 2015 performed at a higher level of efficiency and safety.

As an overall result of the program, significant improvements in accident rates within 12 months after graduation were achieved. MTA calculated what percentage of each graduating class, in three-month increments, did not attend PAT within 12 months after graduation. This "Grad-to-PAT" analysis was used to determine the effectiveness of the bus operator initial orientation and 10-week training program (Table 20-5).

During 2012–2014, the percentages of graduates who did not have to attend PAT within zero to three months after graduation ranged from 75 to 100 percent. In 2015, after the new instructor-student ratio and class size limit were implemented, the percentages were 92.3 to 100 percent. This represents a significant decrease in accidents requiring drivers to attend PAT.

Within three to six months after training, those who graduated in 2012–2014 and did not attend PAT ranged from 66.6 percent to 85.7 percent (not counting 2013). Those who graduated in 2015 ranged from 88.4 percent to 92.8 percent, another notable reduction in accidents.

The financial contribution this initiative has made to MTA's mission is clear. Many employee and customer comments and stories of improved safety, increased customer satisfaction, and improved employee morale have been made public through the media department. All of these add significant evidence that this initiative is also contributing to the fulfillment and potential of employees and satisfaction of riders.

The table of total bus accident claims by year show that the reduction in first-year driver accidents after training has contributed to a significant decrease in claims and related expenditures (Table 20-6).

With its success in reducing the number of new bus operator accidents, the operations training department is now requested to attend executive meetings to identify ways training can be a business partner in achieving agency goals.

MTA now leverages the power of proper training evaluation techniques for agency-wide initiatives to decrease employee absenteeism and improve the customer experience. The MTA team looks forward to analyzing these initiatives using the Kirkpatrick Model and plans to work on developing maintenance training programs and evaluation plans for bus maintenance, light rail maintenance, and Metro maintenance departments.

Table 20-5. Percentage of New Drivers by Graduating Class Who Have Not Attended PAT

Percentage of New Bus Operators By Graduating Class That Have Not Attended PAT

Grad Date	Timeframe		
07/16/12	1) 0-3 Months	78.57%	
	3) 6-12 Months	69.12% / 66.67%	
09/17/12	1) 0-3 Months	76.92%	
	3) 6-12 Months	66.67% / 58.97%	
08/19/13	1) 0-3 Months	100.00%	
	3) 6-12 Months	87.50% / 75.00%	
08/14/14	1) 0-3 Months	76.92%	
	3) 6-12 Months	69.23% / 61.54%	
10/16/14	1) 0-3 Months	75.00%	
	3) 6-12 Months	75.00% / 50.00%	
12/19/14	1) 0-3 Months	85.71%	
	3) 6-12 Months	85.71% / 64.29%	
03/27/15	1) 0-3 Months	100.00%	
	3) 6-12 Months	92.86% / 71.43%	
06/25/15	1) 0-3 Months	96.55%	
	3) 6-12 Months	89.66% / 86.21%	
07/30/15	1) 0-3 Months	92.31%	
	3) 6-12 Months	88.46% / 84.62%	

Percentage of Operators Without PAT — 20.00%, 40.00%, 60.00%, 80.00%, 100.00%

© MTA

Table 20-6. Bus Accident Claims by Year

Fiscal Year	Annual Claims	# of Claims	Average Claim
2011	$5,000,000	1,500	$3,333
2012	$3,000,000	1,073	$2,796
2013	$2,000,000	1,066	$1,876
2014	$1,700,000	1,364	$1,246
2015	$560,000	804	$697

Program Success Factors

The following seven factors contributed significantly to the success of the program:

1. management's active commitment to the usefulness of training evaluation data on all four levels to resolve problems
2. creative points of celebration during and immediately after training
3. lower instructor-student classroom ratios
4. better job aids for bus drivers, as well as opportunities for them to reach out to instructors for post-program assistance and to become union instructors or mentors to new drivers
5. stronger, cooperative relationships with the union to hold bus drivers accountable for poor driving records, including a union-approved 90-day probationary period and a points system
6. new data collection processes in the classroom and on the road that led to data-based decisions to improve initial training and post-accident training
7. improved performance ride check processes and data collection.

Barriers to Success

The following three factors caused initial problems, but due to timely quantitative and qualitative data, corrections were made prior to the program results being jeopardized.

1. Initial resistance to the idea that reducing bus operator class sizes would affect Grad-to-PAT times. After the connections in the data were explained, the program was accepted.

2. The urgency to get bus operators on the street sometimes resulted in instructors not being thorough on the Bus Operator Performance Evaluation Form. With the Bus Operator Performance Report, instructors were briefed on the connection between spending quality time with bus operators and avoiding having to retrain them later in PAT.

3. Inconsistency in grading bus operator performance using the Bus Operator Performance Report. Some retraining of instructors was required, along with emphasizing the criticality of the data gathered.

Summary

The success of this program was largely due to a detailed plan, excellent training, consistent performance support, and targeted evaluation. Additionally, the human factor shone throughout, often coming from the participants themselves. The following story illustrates how the enthusiastic spirit of the training participants provided intangible benefits that cannot be underestimated:

Each bus operator graduation ceremony is a special time for all members of the MTA team, as well as for the graduates and their loved ones. At each graduation, a class representative shares an experience from training and also recognizes those who helped the class along the way. In March 2015, the class representative expressed his appreciation for one particular student who went above and beyond to help a fellow candidate.

The candidate on the receiving end of the friendly gesture was the only student to fail the final exam on the last day of training. The student was given his second and final chance to pass before being let go as an MTA employee. The helpful classmate decided to stay behind for moral support and sit with his classmate as he struggled through the test. He did not want his classmate of 10 weeks to sit alone. Four hours later, the struggling student turned in his exam. The two men waited together as the instructor graded it. He passed! He is now proud to be able to provide for his family as an MTA professional bus operator, and that caring act set the foundation for a career-long friendship.

As the class representative shared this story, the man who had stayed behind to encourage his friend began to cry in front of all the guests and leaders of MTA. The room was so overcome with the display of emotion that everyone was left wiping tears from their eyes.

This story illustrates that training is not just about PowerPoints, manuals, or practical evaluations; it's about changing people's lives for the better.

CHAPTER 21

Coaching Program:
IHC New Zealand

Gail Foster-Bohm, Mark Harris, and David Dewhurst

IHC is New Zealand's largest provider of support for those with an intellectual disability. With approximately 6,000 staff, IHC provides services for 5,000 people, ranging from those living independently to individuals with complex needs. IHC's mission is to advocate for the rights, inclusion, and welfare of all people with an intellectual disability and to support them in leading satisfying lives in their communities. To work toward its mission, IHC has developed a "Strategy 2020" document, which outlines their mission, objectives, and priorities for all stakeholders.

In 2013, IHC embarked on a strategic initiative, the National Coaching Program, to support two training programs with the aim of helping service users become more independent. This supports the "my day, my way" philosophy of self-determination for people with intellectual disability, choosing where and how they live. Developing a coaching culture to support the implementation of these two programs was seen as essential to their success. GMD Partnerships, an affiliate of Kirkpatrick Partners, was chosen to partner with IHC to develop and deliver the coaching program for frontline managers.

The coaching program was initiated in late 2013, and the pilot was launched in three regions. Due to the results of the pilot, centralization of shared administrative services, and introduction of the EPiC performance development framework in 2014, changes to the coaching program were required. The EPiC framework is based on "expectations, people, and conversations," and has two main principles: 1) "as and when required," as opposed to an annual appraisal, and 2) "mutual responsibility."

The EPiC framework contains four main elements: 1) outcomes, 2) positive feedback, 3) correction, and 4) personal development.

Following the final trial, which was held in late 2014, a national rollout of the program began in 2015, with completion expected in mid-2016.

Stakeholder Expectations

Stakeholder expectations focused on implementing the IHC 2020 Strategy and the EPiC framework. In discussions with L&D and program facilitators, stakeholders said that service managers should spend more time coaching frontline service staff to be capable, confident, and committed professionals who could support service users in learning new skills and trying new things. They believed this would help them to lead fulfilling lives, following the "my day, my way" philosophy.

Critical Behaviors

Managers who graduate from the coaching training program are expected to coach their support service staff consistent with the EPiC framework, using tools and techniques obtained during the program. This means that they need to hold regular conversations one-on-one with staff and complete 7-, 30-, and 60-day coaching sessions. Managers are required to use the personality profiling tool introduced during the program to understand the strengths and potential blind spots of each team member and adjust their own leadership style accordingly.

Project Methodology

The program followed the New World Kirkpatrick Model. After an initial determination of needs, stakeholder expectations were defined. From there, critical behaviors and leading indicators were identified. The coaching program and related evaluation methods and tools were developed. The resulting two-day coaching program was piloted in three regions.

Evaluation data were analyzed and used to modify the program; the revised program was piloted. The program data were reviewed in a series of meetings, and the program was finalized for national rollout.

During the rollout, evaluation continued so that data could be reviewed continuously to ensure that the program was on track to meet its goals.

Evaluation Methods

During the pilot, formative evaluation ensured that participants were comfortable and engaged, and that they had received guidance to help them see the relevance of what they were learning. Reaction, learning, and predictive behavior (Levels 1–3) were evaluated at the end of the workshop using a customized reaction sheet (Table 21-1).

Graduating participants were asked to complete an action plan diary using the following questions:

- As a result of what I've learned today, what do I need to start doing?
- As a result of what I've learned today, what do I need to stop doing?
- As a result of what I've learned today, what do I need to continue doing?
- What have we covered today that I need to think some more about?
- On a scale of 1–5, how confident are you that you will be able to carry out what you have learned back on the job?
- On a scale of 1–5, how committed are you that you will be able to carry out what you have learned back on the job?

The learning and development consultant made phone calls to managers 60 days after the program, asking, "What did you learn and how are you using the tools and techniques taught?"

Face-to-face interviews were held with managers to ask:

- What is working? Why?
- What is not working? Why?
- What is changing?

Face-to-face meetings were held with support workers to ask:

- What is different now in the way your manager is operating compared to before the coaching program?
- How has your manager been supporting you since the program?
- What results are you seeing?

A questionnaire was provided to the participants of the pilot program to identify contributing factors to the success of the coaching practice for service managers. It asked the following questions:

- What progress has the participant made in coaching xxx?
- Who else has he or she been coaching?

Table 21-1. Post-Program Reaction Sheet

Program: Coaching Skills for Service Managers and Senior Support Workers

My manager met with me to discuss the program prior to attending the workshop and we worked through the Before the Workshop section of my Action Planning Diary (please circle):

| Yes | No |

- For questions 1–7, please use the following scale:
  1 = strongly disagree   10 = strongly agree
- Please circle the appropriate rating.
- Please provide any comments to explain your rating.

Strongly
disagree
Strongly
agree
1 2 3 4 5 6 7 8 9 10   1. I received helpful information prior to attending the workshop.
Comments:

Strongly
disagree
Strongly
agree
1 2 3 4 5 6 7 8 9 10   2. I took responsibility for being involved in the workshop.
Comments:

Strongly
disagree
Strongly
agree
1 2 3 4 5 6 7 8 9 10   3. I understand how to apply what I learned on the job.
Comments:

Strongly
disagree
Strongly
agree
1 2 3 4 5 6 7 8 9 10   4. What I learned in this workshop will help me on the job.
Comments:

Strongly
disagree
Strongly
agree
1 2 3 4 5 6 7 8 9 10   5. The workshop material will be helpful on the job.
Comments:

Strongly
disagree
Strongly
agree
1 2 3 4 5 6 7 8 9 10   6. The presentation style of the facilitator contributed to my learning experience.
Comments:

Strongly
disagree
Strongly
agree
1 2 3 4 5 6 7 8 9 10   7. I believe I will see an impact in the following areas as I apply
1 2 3 4 5 6 7 8 9 10   what I have learned:
1 2 3 4 5 6 7 8 9 10   • Stronger relationships with staff members
                                   • People we support are actively engaged in fulfilling activities
                                   • Increase in quality outcomes for people we support
Comments:

Please turn over:

Table 21-1. Post-Program Reaction Sheet *(continued)*

Program: Coaching Skills for Service Managers and Senior Support Workers

- For questions 8–10, please use the following scale:

1	2	3	4	5
None or very low level				Very high level

- Please circle the appropriate rating.
- Please provide any comments to explain your rating.

Before the workshop		After the workshop

1 2 3 4 5   **8. Knowledge of the skills required to coach**   1 2 3 4 5

If you rated your "after the course" knowledge at 3 or less, what needs to happen to increase your knowledge?

_____

1 2 3 4 5   **9. Confidence to coach team members**   1 2 3 4 5

If you rated your "after the course" confidence at 3 or less, what needs to happen to increase your confidence?

_____

1 2 3 4 5   **10. Commitment to coach team members**   1 2 3 4 5

If you rated your "after the course" commitment at 3 or less, what needs to happen to increase your commitment?

_____

11. How can this program be improved?

_____

_____

12. Please share any additional comments you wish to make. If you wish to authorize us to use your comments in GMD Partnerships marketing materials, please print your name and organization name.

_____

_____

Thank you.

- What specific coaching behaviors are you seeing?
- How is the participant's coaching helping the support worker? What else is helping the support worker so that his or her coaching is effective?
- What is the participant struggling with in coaching the support worker?
- How is this affecting the service user?

Key data from the pilot were reported in a dashboard (Table 21-2).

The summation of this data was used to establish changes to the final rollout of the program.

All programs after the pilot were evaluated using the same evaluation form at the end. The results of these evaluations were analyzed and e-mailed to the general manager, area manager, and learning and development team with suggested actions based on the data.

Data on Level 3, on-the-job behaviors, and Level 4, leading indicators, were also gathered during 30-, 60-, 90-, and 120-day post-workshop catch-up calls between the facilitator and the area manager. Although not consistent, a simple spreadsheet is being adopted to capture the progress of each attendee based on their actions from 0 to 120 days post-workshop, for presentation to the IHC senior management team with recommendations for sustaining the results of the program in the future.

Key Findings and Results

Positive behavioral change was noted at 30 days after the workshop, and fully evident at 60 days. Consistent execution of the critical behaviors since training has yielded valuable results. As hoped, managers are coaching staff consistently using the EPiC methods and using the tools and techniques they learned in training. They have used the personality profiling tool to better understand their team members and adjust their leadership style accordingly. Managers are holding regular, effective conversations with staff one on one and in team meetings, and completing 7-, 30-, and 60-day post-workshop coaching sessions with their staffs.

Approximately 85 percent of managers indicated they were spending more time with their staff and service users and all managers interviewed indicated they were coaching and mentoring staff more, specifically so that staff could better support service users.

Process changes have been implemented to better support service users, who, in turn, are being given opportunities to attend different day-based activities not previously provided. As a result, there has been an increase in service users achieving personal goals with staff support.

Table 21-2. Pilot Program Dashboard

Key Measurement	Targeted % of Managers	Actual	Status
Managers spend more time in services coaching team members to support service users	100%	100%	→
Managers provide more support to help staff do their jobs	80%	70%	↑
Work smart so we can free up staff and resources to work with people	80%	65%	↑
EPiC approach reflected in the way managers develop and support staff	80%	75%	↑
Managers trying new ways of doing things	80%	90%	↑
Managers use of information from the profiling tool	100%	70%	→
Managers use of the coaching tools provided in the workshop	80%	90%	↑

Compared to target		Compared to previous month	
At or above	⬤	Better	↑
Somewhat below	⬤	Same	→
Significantly below	⬤	Worse	↓

©IHC New Zealand

Unexpected Benefits

In addition to the anticipated program outcomes, there have been unexpected benefits in the areas of communication and effective relationship building. Here are some specifics:

- Conflict resolution has occurred in many service areas, and in all cases has aligned to the use and understanding of the profiling tools used in the workshop.
- Seventy-eight percent of program participants feel their teams are working better together, solving problems, and providing better services for service users. For example, one participant stated, "My worst critic has had a complete turnaround and is offering to do extra tasks." Another commented, "There has been a significant change in how I am interacting with my team. I am listening differently, not so quick to interject, and communicating in such a way that solutions are coming from the support workers themselves. This is generating more conversation and empowering staff."
- Questions involving mutual responsibility are now used: "How should we approach this?" "What do we all think about this?" "How do we resolve this issue?" Before the coaching workshop, commands were common.

Success Stories

The most exciting data, however, come from the service users who have benefited from improved assistance as a result of the coaching their service providers have received. These are just a few of the success stories. (Names have been changed to protect privacy.)

1. Betty is a service user in her late 50s who has Down syndrome. She is quiet and struggles to say what she wants. Her goal is to be able to do scrapbooking as a hobby. Her support worker, Tia, has learned through coaching from her manager, Linda, how to communicate with Betty so that Betty speaks up. Tia herself has become more confident in supporting Betty, who is now actively scrapbooking.

2. Janee is a service user in her early 30s who has a mild intellectual disability. Food and eating overwhelm her, and she has become obese. She works three mornings a week filling shelves in a local supermarket, and she is struggling on the job because of her weight and lack of fitness. Janee has personal goals to lose weight and become more physically fit. Key to this is making informed choices as to what to eat and at what times to eat. Paula, an experienced manager, and her two support

workers developed a visual food board with Janee to help her make healthy food choices. The first meeting with Janee was a disaster—the support workers disagreed in front of Janee on how best to support her. This soured Janee on using the visual food board. Paula used her coaching skills to help the support workers understand that they needed to put Janee first and foremost and to not let their personal values get in the way. They went back to Janee for a second meeting during which they agreed on how to support her. They are meeting regularly, and Janee is now using the visual food board. Her health and well-being have improved, and she is able to do her job at the supermarket better.

3. James, a service user with IHC for five years, is in his 20s, autistic, and has a tendency to self-harm. His support worker, with coaching from the service manager, has become more adept at identifying the triggers that cause James's self-harm. As a consequence, James has stopped self-harming, has become a more positive person, is able to go out, visit the local IHC office, and interact with more IHC staff.

4. Anne is a service user in her 50s who has been supported by IHC and other providers for 30 years. She lives in a flat and is supported by IHC to live as independently as possible. Historically, Anne's family has managed her money for her, but the goal is for Anne to manage her own money with the help of IHC and her support worker, Liz. Liz has used listening and questioning skills with Anne to help her withdraw money from the bank and to learn how to interact with the bank teller. Anne is now able to stand patiently in a queue, sign her name to withdraw cash, ask for the denominations of bank notes she would like, and thank the bank teller. As a result, Anne's confidence and social skills have grown noticeably. "By the end of the interaction with the bank teller, Anne has grown in stature by six inches," says Liz.

5. Melody is in her late 40s, has both physical and medium-level intellectual disabilities, and is supported by Sharma. Melody had been requesting changes to the services she was receiving, because she was getting bored. Previously, she would be given options to try. However, now Sharma uses techniques provided in the coaching program to establish what Melody would like to try; she persuaded Melody to think about the options and make her own decision. Following this, Melody experienced anxiety because she was losing or forgetting her personal belongings. Sharma asked Melody how she could take responsibility for her own belongings and got her to think about the options and consequences of each. Melody came to a conclusion, put it into practice, and there has not been an issue since. This has taken away the anxiety for Melody and given her a sense of pride.

Success Factors

The success factors rated highest by managers who participated in this initiative indicate that the program itself, support from their peers, and their own personal determination were the top factors in their success as coaches for the support workers, followed by support from the learning and development team (Table 21-3). Support from their managers (area managers) and a good system of accountability rated somewhat lower.

Table 21-3. Coaching Program Success Factors

The reason for the success you have had in your coaching practice is:

Factor	Rating
The Training Program	4.2
Coaching From Your Manager	3.0
Team Meetings	3.0
Manager Support	3.0
Support From Your Peers	4.0
Support From L&D	3.6
System of Accountability	3.2
Your Personal Determination	4.2

0 = Little Contribution, 5 = Significant Contribution

© *IHC New Zealand*

Barriers to Success

There were several barriers to success, all of which could be remedied by making specific internal adjustments, which are noted here.

Barrier to Success #1

During the pilot, the wrong participants were selected in some cases. On several occasions, participant level of competency was not of the caliber required to successfully grasp the concepts delivered in the workshop or to apply them on the job.

Adjustment made: L&D worked with area managers to select participants who had the necessary experience and ability to implement the new learning.

Barrier to Success #2

Participants did not understand why they were going to the training, and what was expected of them in some cases. In these cases, no pre-workshop meeting had occurred between the manager and team members.

Adjustments made: General manager and area manager pre-rollout workshops were held to ensure they understood the importance of their roles in the program, and the importance of making time to understand and discuss the process with their team members. Greater accountability was placed on area managers to ensure pre- and post-workshop meetings were held.

Barrier to Success #3

Work pressures and other initiatives sometimes took precedence over the program. It became clear during the trials that when other initiatives were introduced or when workloads increased, commitment levels dropped and post-workshop coaching sessions did not take place.

Adjustment made: L&D acknowledged the conflicting priorities and ensured that each area was "training ready." Unplanned priority changes proved more difficult and required flexibility in program delivery.

Barrier to Success #4

During the rollout, administrative logistics increased significantly without sufficient planning.

Adjustment made: Administrative tasks were realigned and an L&D consultant was made available to support each area manager at the time of their program.

Barrier to Success #5

In some cases, changing the behaviors of long-standing staff proved difficult.

Adjustment made: Coaching was used as a tactic to support these staff in viewing ways of supporting service users not previously considered. This is an ongoing issue that has come up in each area, but we are seeing some movement.

Recommendations

It has been a great experience learning from the rollout of this coaching program and seeing the direct impact it has had in enhancing the lives of the people we support. Based on this learning, we offer the following findings and recommendations:

1. The pre-workshop briefings with the general managers and area managers proved critical to the success of the program. This was a new process for IHC and should be replicated for other mission-critical programs.

2. Area managers should be prepared not only for the workshop (and their role in the process), but also for their coaching sessions for this program and other mission-critical initiatives in the future.

3. The L&D team should work sufficiently in the business during the rollout. For example, they should attend pre-workshop meetings and the workshops themselves, and conduct post-workshop coaching, informal chats, formal interviews, and evaluation.

4. Continue to ensure that strong administrative processes are in place to support similar programs of this size.

5. Continue to monitor and adjust after pilot deliveries and the main rollout to ensure that the program does not lose momentum or linkage to current initiatives.

6. Continue on-the-job support, especially from area managers, to keep the learning and coaching practice alive. Where this support has occurred, there is evidence of enhanced coaching practice.

Summary

The approach taken to implement the National Coaching Program has differed from any program rolled out previously within IHC. The use of a comprehensive program with pre- and post-workshop support and accountability rather than just a workshop approach has been a first. From an operational perspective, the business accepted the need for this and has, in most areas, embraced this approach.

It is gratifying that once expectations were outlined, IHC staff took responsibility for their learning, and the majority of participants have really tried to put their new learning into practice.

Summative evaluation and observation has shown that managers are working in services more and spending more time working alongside their teams. This is a critical factor in delivering better service to the people IHC supports.

There has been a significant shift in the way managers work. Some areas are working more effectively than others, as are individuals; however, positive change has occurred at all levels of capability. The challenge is to ensure the program continues to be monitored and adjusted as required, and that each new strategic initiative follows a similar approach. In this way, we will ensure that the lives of our users are enhanced—"my day, my way."

Call to Action

Given the current economic climate in which all expenditures are being carefully monitored, there is no better time to use the four levels to create, deliver, measure, and validate training that has true organizational value. It is time to put old and even revered practices away. No more "smile sheets, pre- and post-tests, and hope for the best." It is time to drive and leverage training and post-training support and accountability to maximize performance and results. It is time to be strategic business partners. Failing to do so will likely lead to our replacement by YouTube, apps, and avatars.

There is also no better time to create a new standard within the learning industry. Stakeholders in business, government, the military, and not-for-profits are all seeking cost-effective ways to strengthen business and mission accomplishment. Most are looking to make a difference. We believe the New World Kirkpatrick Model grants an opportunity to provide just that.

Allow us to explain with a personal story. We had a cement walk leading to the front door of our first home after we got married. As Jim was walking up the path shortly after we moved in, he noticed that the former owners had depressed the footprints of (we assume) their small child and carved his or her initials into the sidewalk. Upon discovering this legacy, Jim was somewhat envious that these former homeowners had been able to leave their mark. He wanted to do the same, but he knew he would have to find his own fresh cement.

The good news is that you are not too late to leave your mark in the learning industry, as an individual or a team. The cement is wet. During this time of economic challenge, when our industry is under fire, the good news is that business leaders—our jury members—are looking anywhere and everywhere for solutions to their incredible challenges. We have the unique opportunity to provide significant answers for them, and to carve out a new learning legacy by becoming true strategic business partners. Fortunately, these economic times won't last forever. This creates a limited-time window and urgency for you to take action before the "cement dries" in the training and business world.

Your Personal Action Plan

Not sure where to start? Start with deciding to disrupt tradition by focusing on truth. A foundation belief of this model is that evaluation has to be about truth, not about patting the backs of instructional designers, event organizers, and trainers. Surveys alone uncover only a portion of what is actually happening in the classroom and beyond. Oftentimes, survey results have little to do with truth at all. Start by modifying your pre- and post-training conversations, your evaluation tools and methods, and your analysis and recommendations to reflect truth. It is only through truthful evaluation that your organization can make effective decisions, maximize results, and ultimately earn the trust of stakeholders.

As a call to action, why don't you put the Kirkpatrick Model to personal use in the following way? We would like each of you to target a program coming up within the next year that could benefit from the application of the concepts in this book. Choose a program that is major enough that you can use what you have learned. Let your approach be humble of personal ego but bold in spirit for the mission. Be a bright light. Let your program illuminate the learning and performance path up the mountain to business results so others will follow.

References

Brinkerhoff, R.O. 2003. *The Success Case Method: Find Out Quickly What's Working and What's Not*. San Francisco, CA: Berrett-Koehler.

Champagne, M.V. 2014. *The Survey Playbook: Volume 1: How to Create the Perfect Survey*.

Kirkpatrick, J.D., and W.K. Kirkpatrick. 2015. "The Four Levels of Evaluation—An Update." *TD at Work*. Alexandria, VA: ATD Press.

———. 2013. *Bringing Business Partnership to Life: The Story of the Brunei Window Washer*. St. Louis, MO: Kirkpatrick Publishing.

———. 2010. *Training on Trial: How Workplace Learning Must Reinvent Itself to Remain Relevant*. New York: AMACOM.

———. 2009. *Kirkpatrick Then and Now: A Strong Foundation for the Future*. St. Louis, MO: Kirkpatrick Publishing.

About the Authors

Dr. Jim Kirkpatrick and Wendy Kayser Kirkpatrick are co-owners of Kirkpatrick Partners. Together, they carry on the work of Jim's late father, Dr. Don Kirkpatrick, who served as the company's honorary chairman until his passing in May 2014.

Don created what later became known as the Kirkpatrick Model in the mid-1950s as part of his PhD dissertation. His goal was to effectively measure the impact of the management development programs he was teaching at the University of Wisconsin Management Institute. In 1959, Don first published his thoughts on training evaluation with a series of four articles in the *Journal of the American Society of Training Directors* entitled "Reaction," "Learning," "Behavior," and "Results," respectively.

After several years in the corporate world, Don returned to the University of Wisconsin, where he spent the remainder of his career as a professor. He published numerous books, served as the president of ASTD, and received various lifetime achievement awards, as well as a thought leadership award and induction into *Training* magazine's Hall of Fame.

Jim is a thought leader and change driver in training evaluation and the creator of the New World Kirkpatrick Model. Using his 15 years of experience in the corporate world, including eight years as a corporate training manager, Jim trains and consults for corporate, government, military, and humanitarian organizations around the world. He is passionate about assisting learning professionals in redefining themselves as strategic business partners to become a viable force in the workplace.

Jim delivers lively keynote addresses and conducts workshops on topics including using evaluation to help execute business strategy, building and leveraging business partnerships, increasing the transfer of learning to on-the-job behaviors, and maximizing business results.

Wendy is a global driving force of the use and implementation of the Kirkpatrick Model, leading companies to measurable success through training and evaluation.

Wendy's results orientation stems from more than two decades of business experience in retailing, marketing, and training. She has held positions as a buyer, product manager, process manager, and training manager, which leveraged her ability to organize complex, multifaceted projects and yield rapid results. As a training manager, she managed the training curriculum for 1,500 sales and customer service representatives across North America.

Wendy is a recipient of the 2013 Emerging Training Leaders Award from *Training* magazine.

Jim and Wendy have written three books, including *Training on Trial: How Workplace Learning Must Reinvent Itself to Remain Relevant*, and have also served as the subject matter experts for the United States Office of Personnel Management's *Training Evaluation Field Guide: Demonstrating the Value of Training at Every Level*.

When they are not working, Jim can be found on his boat fishing with his friends; Wendy alternately increases and decreases her carbon footprint with decorating projects in their home and conservation activities such as composting, recycling, and repurposing. Read more about the Kirkpatricks at kirkpatrickpartners.com.

About the Contributors

Paul Aggett is the learning and development manager for Greencore Foods, Northampton, United Kingdom. With over 20 years' experience in development, he has a passion for developing programs that help unleash people's latent talent and deliver tangible business results.

Paul Beech is the manager of Emirates Global Contact Center, Dubai, United Arab Emirates.

Karen Bell-Wright is senior vice president of Emirates Global Contact and Retail Centers, Dubai, United Arab Emirates.

Robert O. Brinkerhoff is an internationally recognized expert in training effectiveness and evaluation and the principal architect of the Advantage Way. A professor emeritus at Western Michigan University, where he was responsible for graduate programs in human resource management, Brinkerhoff earned his doctorate in program evaluation at the University of Virginia. He is the author of *Telling Training's Story: Evaluation Made Simple, Credible, and Effective* (2006); *The Success Case Method: Find Out Quickly What's Working and What's Not* (2003); co-author with Anne M. Apking of *High Impact Learning: Strategies for Leveraging Performance and Business Results from Training Investments* (2001); and co-author with Timothy P. Mooney of *Courageous Training: Bold Actions for Business Results* (2008).

Saul Carliner is an associate professor and provost's e-learning fellow at Concordia University in Montreal, where he also directs the doctoral program in education. His research and teaching focus on the design of materials for learning and communication in the workplace, the management of groups that produce these materials, and the transfer of research to practice. He also serves as director of research for Lakewood Media. As a consultant, Carliner has advised organizations such as Alltel Wireless, Bronx Zoo, Equitas, IBM, Lowe's, ST Microelectronics, and several U.S. and Canadian government agencies on complex design projects and strategic issues in management and evaluation. Among his eight books are *Informal Learning Basics* (2012) and *Training Design Basics* (2nd edition, 2015).

Matthew Champagne is director of research at Embedded Assessments and has served as a senior research fellow, university professor, evaluator, consultant, and entrepreneur. He founded the IDEA Lab, the first laboratory dedicated to the assessment of web-based learning, and his research and practice in developing and evaluating large-scale online learning programs has influenced assessment practices in higher education and industry since the mid-1990s. He has advised and helped implement online course evaluation systems at 370 colleges and learning organizations and is the author of 50 articles and how-to guides on effectively using student feedback and embedded assessment technology to improve teaching and learning. Dr. Champagne earned his doctorate and master's degrees in psychology from Purdue University.

David Dewhurst is a co-founder, leadership coach, and facilitator with GMD Partnerships, a leadership development company dedicated to seeing organizations achieve their business results through effective changes in leadership behavior. He is passionate about coaching and preparing leaders to obtain better business results. With Mark Harris, he presents at multiple international conferences and webinars and has co-authored published articles on the implementation of the Kirkpatrick methods and tools for improving business; they are the Australasian affiliates for Kirkpatrick Partners.

Joyce Donohoe is the manager of Emirates Strategic Commercial and Service Initiatives, Group Learning and Development, at Emirates Airline, Dubai, United Arab Emirates.

Gail Foster-Bohm is the owner of GFB Learning and Development, a company specializing in identifying learning and development needs and providing effective solutions. She has assisted multiple organizations to realize effective transfer of learning to on-the-job behavior.

Mark Harris is co-founder, leadership coach, and facilitator with GMD Partnerships. He is dedicated to helping organizations implement learning solutions that help accelerate business strategy. With David Dewhurst, he has presented at multiple international conferences and webinars and is co-author of several published articles on the implementation of the Kirkpatrick methods and tools for improving business; they are the Australasian affiliates for Kirkpatrick Partners.

William Horton is an e-learning specialist and president of William Horton Consulting. He has been designing technology-based training since 1971 when, as an undergraduate, he designed a network-based course for the Massachusetts Institute of Technology's Center for Advanced Engineering Study. He is the author of numerous books, including *E-Learning by Design* (2nd edition, 2011) and *Evaluating E-Learning* (2006).

Andrew Jefferson is co-founder and chief executive officer of the 6Ds Company, a training and consulting firm dedicated to helping companies maximize the return on their investments in training and development. He is also a frequent and popular presenter and consultant who views learning as a critical source of competitive advantage in an increasingly knowledge-based economy. He is co-author with Roy Pollock of *Getting Your Money's Worth from Training and Development* (2009), *The Six Disciplines of Breakthrough Learning: How to Turn Training and Development into Business Results* (2015), and *The Field Guide to the 6Ds: How to Use the Six Disciplines to Transform Learning into Business Results* (2014).

Timothy P. Mooney is a partner with the Advantage Performance Group. Prior to joining Advantage, he served in a senior management capacity for DDI, working closely with leading global organizations. In addition, he has more than 25 years of corporate sales management and consulting experience. He holds a bachelor's degree in psychology from Butler University and a master's degree in industrial/organizational psychology from the University of Akron. He is co-author with Robert O. Brinkerhoff of *Courageous Training: Bold Actions for Business Results* (2008).

Roy Pollock is the co-founder and chief learning officer of the 6Ds Company. With a passion for helping individuals and teams succeed, he is a popular international speaker and consultant on improving the value created by training and development. He is the co-author with Andrew Jefferson of *Getting Your Money's Worth from Training and Development* (2009), *The Six Disciplines of Breakthrough Learning: How to Turn Training and Development into Business Results* (2015), and *The Field Guide to the 6Ds: How to Use the Six Disciplines to Transform Learning into Business Results* (2014).

Clark Quinn helps organizations align their use of technology with how people think, work, and learn. With a PhD in cognition and more than 35 years designing learning technology systems and solutions, he is the author of numerous articles, chapters, and four books, including *Designing mLearning: Tapping into the Mobile Revolution for Organizational Performance* (2011). He consults and speaks around the globe, and in 2012 he was awarded the eLearning Guild's Guild Master award.

Linn Steer is Academy Director (EMEA) of the Getinge Group and is responsible for all learning and development related activities for employees, distributors, and customers in Europe, the Middle East, and Africa. For the last 18 years, she has worked in various marketing, business, and sales development positions within the medical device industry. In 2012, she began to develop the ArjoHuntleigh Academy and since then her focus has been to develop sales force capabilities in line with business needs. She holds degrees in physiotherapy and business administration with a focus on finance and marketing. She is also a Gold Level Certified Kirkpatrick professional.

Michael Wiedecker is the director of training and development for the Maryland Transit Administration (MTA), one of the largest multimodal transit systems in the United States. After serving in the U.S. Navy, he began a rewarding career in the transportation industry and over the past 29 years has held several positions at MTA, including technician, instructor, manager of safety training, light rail project manager, and deputy director of light rail operations. He has been a guest speaker at conferences, the Training Officers Consortium, and his local chapter of ATD; other transit properties have sought out his advice in training evaluation best practices.

Index